CW00506462

BRANDING SECRETS

THE UNDERGROUND PLAYBOOK FOR BUILDING A GREAT BRAND WITH VERY LITTLE MONEY

Kevin Albert

ISBN 979-8704937883

To my parents,
whose values helped me forge my own personal brand.

CONTENTS

Foreword

I met Kevin at a branding workshop that had been organized for small business owners and entrepreneurs on the Spanish coast of the Mediterranean. From the first minute I was struck by the concept he presented in his talk, differentiating himself from the other expert speakers: **the possibility of creating an awesome brand with limited funds**. I am one of those people who always thinks there must be other ways of doing things, that the "little guy" can compete with or even do better than the corporate giants, and that was the vision Kevin transmitted over the course of the conference: the size of your business doesn't matter – **you can and should create a GREAT BRAND**.

Many of us want to earn a living for ourselves or grow our businesses, and being able to distinguish ourselves, stand out, and position ourselves in the same way as large brands do will enable us to achieve our goals much more quickly.

The success of a good brand, and in turn of a good business, lies in laying stable foundations. This is done by clearly setting out the brand's mission, vision and values from the very start, and through a thorough understanding of the target client profile. When one of these building blocks is missing, the chances of business success or continuity are dramatically reduced. To paraphrase Lewis Carroll, *"when you don't know where you're going, the road you take won't matter"*.

A different manual was needed, one not aimed at students of branding, but one which spoke of creating a brand from the perspective of the transparency, clarity and honesty required to debunk the myth that "branding is expensive".

This book will help you, in a practical and realistic way, to create a powerful brand with minimal investment. Whether you're an entrepreneur, you want to become one, or you own your own business, I can't think of any reason why you *wouldn't* want to build your brand, especially knowing that you can do so for far less money that you probably realize.

Don't be scared off, you don't have to become an overnight expert in each and every one of the fields necessary to create a brand. That couldn't be further from the truth.

This book will guide you step-by-step through the process of creating your brand, showing you which areas you need to work on yourself, directly, and which are better to outsource; how to handle everything; and what is needed if you are to reduce your costs by up to 80% of what you would pay a branding agency.

Enjoy the book, read it carefully and make the most of the knowledge and experience Kevin has poured into these pages, to help *you* to build *your* brand without giving yourself a heart attack.

Ana Escudero
Digital Strategy Consultant
Co-founder of Yuvalia

Warnings, promises and commitments

Warning

This is NOT a "do-it-yourself" manual. Although later on you'll see that there are certain times where I do recommend that entrepreneurs takes on the responsibility for certain tasks related to creating their brand for themselves, my overriding mission with this book is that you **learn to outsource in an intelligent way.**

Promise

In this book I'll show you how to reduce a quote of between $30,000 to $60,000, which is what any run – of-the-mill branding agency would quote you to create the basic features of your brand, to **less than $1,000.** All without losing a single shred of quality!

Commitment

As I state in this book's description, and repeat here now, if I'm not successful in **reducing your costs by at least 80%** compared to what you've previously been quoted by any agencies you may have consulted, you have my solemn word that **I will reimburse the full price of your purchase**.

Introduction

1.1. The idea.

The idea behind writing this book came to me in 2012 when, during one of my MBA classes at the University of Alicante, Fernando Olivares, professor of Business Image and Identity, was explaining the various branding strategies employed by businesses and how some of these strategies were generally reserved for companies with an annual turnover of $40m or more.

Forty millions! Were all of the students sitting in that hall with me really aspiring to – or able to – manage a business of such proportions? It was even more absurd given that, with the economic status we all found ourselves in at the time, it would be enough of a miracle if those self-same businesses employed us as cashiers, shelf stackers or interns.

My own personal reason for studying the MBA was to arm myself with all of the tools necessary to realize my own projects (which were and are numerous and varied), with the aim of increasing their chances of success.

Did Fernando mean that managing our own identities would have to be left till later? That us entrepreneurs needn't worry about the image projected by our company at first, or that branding was only something for big business?

Of course not! And I knew as much. From the moment I began my journey as an entrepreneur back in 2004, I have come across a variety of tools and learned numerous strategies that aren't taught on any MBA – for many reasons that I won't go into here, as they would take up a whole other book – which allow any entrepreneur to create a great brand regardless of their annual turnover.

Based on my own personal experiences, I decided to carry out some research, which lasted for over 4 years and which I currently still add to and update, with the aim of discovering new and/or better ways to manage each and every aspect of building a great brand at a low, low price, if not for free.

I hope that everything I have discovered during my research, and which is captured here in this book, is as fascinating for you as it has been for me. I hope it spurs you on and above all, helps you to create a powerful brand that takes you a few steps closer to realizing your business dreams.

1.2. The research.

To give you a bit of background and show you how I went about performing this research, which led me to discover how to create a low cost brand, I'd like to explain the 4 steps that made up the process:

A. Reviewing books.
B. Interviewing entrepreneurs.
C. Attending events about branding.
D. Google searches.

A. Reviewing books.

The first step in my research was to find out if there were already any books dealing with the topic I wanted to address.

However, all of the books I found on branding were purely theoretical, written only with big business in mind (even when their titles suggested otherwise) and aimed at either students of the subject or branding professionals.

In my opinion one of the reasons for this is the lack of importance which, until now, has been attached to brand management in terms of the global success of a business, and because branding has generally been a subject dealt with only in university circles.

The boom of entrepreneurship, the ease of creating a startup thanks to the Internet, and the endless technological tools available to us make it necessary – now more than ever – for brands to stand out ahead of their competitors.

In this context, creating **a powerful brand** becomes a necessity for entrepreneurs, independent professionals and SMEs.

If you'd like to learn more about the history of branding, delve into its terminology, or discover new theories proposed by self-proclaimed "branding gurus", you will easily find 100s of books on the subject. However, if you're a business person or entrepreneur and what really interests you is creating your brand without investing vast sums of money, then this is the book for you.

B. Interviewing entrepreneurs.

The next step was to search for businesses and entrepreneurs who fulfilled one sole requirement: having created a recognized brand on limited economic resources.

When it came to choosing my interviewees, I searched among the winners and participants of various competitions for young entrepreneurs organized and held on an international scale over previous years.

Once I'd chosen them, I would get in touch to explain my project and request a face to face interview, or via video conference, and most of them were happy to oblige.

I have to admit that I really enjoyed these interviews and I met some wonderful people with whom, surprisingly, I had more in common than many of my lifelong friends.

As I completed the interviews, I realized that although each interviewee posed themselves as "low cost", that wasn't always strictly the truth. In fact less than 10% of the entrepreneurs I interviewed met the requirements I had set out, while the rest in reality had considerably more equity at their disposal: some because they were from a rich family, others because they already owned other businesses, others still because they had sought external investment. None of this diminishes their merit in the slightest, but they were sadly no longer useful to my research as they didn't fit in with the type of entrepreneur – the profile – that I was looking for. Given they had sufficient money to back them, why would they waste time searching for low cost strategies and tools? To illustrate with a couple examples: one of these "entrepreneurs" had spent more on the design of his logo ($2,000), and another on registering his brand ($1,000) than I propose to spend on the entire branding strategy, including, among other things, logo design and trademark registration.

Although I was able to take away more or less valuable lessons from each company interviewed, I saw with my own eyes that the businesses that had strong financial backing did things very differently from those whose budget was closer to $0. The latter are the ones that, without a doubt, afforded me the most relevant information with which to craft my book.

During the course of these interviews, I discovered a strange thing that helped me understand why nobody had written this book until now. Among those entrepreneurs that had created their brand using very limited resources, there were very few willing to disclose their "secrets", attributing much of their success to these.

An example of this is outlined below, and came up in the first interview I carried out:

- No way, not without a confidentiality agreement. I would be grateful if you would abstain from recording the interview. I'm sure we're not the only ones to request as much.
- In fact - I replied - my colleagues have met with the Head of Communications from companies such as BBVA and Inditex, and they had no such issues.
- Of course not, such large companies have no issue with sharing how they do what they do, because no one can afford to copy them and compete with them. But our know-how is our most valued resource, and we have no plans to share it - he concluded -

C. Attending events on branding.

The third step in my research was aimed at amassing the largest number of useful tools mentioned at any events or training activities on branding.

During the course of my investigations I became virtually addicted to these types of event and I attended every course, workshop, conference, etc. on branding, as well as other related topics, that I could find, and which I deemed enriching for my research and book.

As with the interviews of entrepreneurs, I genuinely enjoyed these events, meeting incredible people and forging solid friendships, sharing my concerns and being made to feel slightly more normal in a world which, until this point, seemed to be completely up against me. If you're an entrepreneur and you're frustrated that your family and friends don't see things your way, and think that you're a bit weird, then you'll take to such events like a duck to water.

Unfortunately, I would have to say this was the main benefit of attending so many of these events, because even though you come away from some of them with a few tools or strategies to help you manage your brand more efficiently, many of them (especially the free ones) have an entirely different agenda.

I was to discover that such events are used by branding agencies and professionals as an excellent means of acquiring new clients. Which in principle is fine, if it weren't for the fact that to gain as many new clients as possible, it's vital to ensure the attendees don't learn too much, or anything at all, during the event itself. The most common formula is to present some strategies, actions or tasks required to create a successful brand (SEO, social media etc.) in such a complicated, technical way that you arrive at the logical conclusion that the best thing to do would be to contract the services of a professional instead of doing things for yourself!

I'm not criticizing the recommendation that certain things are best left to the experts. I wholeheartedly agree with that. Good brand management does not require you to learn to do everything yourself, not even close. What I'm criticizing here is that, if the idea behind these events isn't to teach something, they shouldn't be presented as training sessions where you can *"learn to..."*, *"find out all you need to know about..."* and other common ways of describing the supposed benefits of attending such activities.

Although this seemed pretty obvious to me by that point, I decided to check one final time. To this end, I got in touch with the organizers of a few conferences (both free and paying), offering myself as an expert speaker on branding and indicating that I was in the process of finalizing my book on the very subject. All of the organizers welcomed my proposal with open arms – at least to begin with. Unfortunately, further down the line when I hinted I would comment on and analyze the tools I'll be teaching you to use in this book, I was quickly, and fairly rudely, ruled out as a speaker.

The phrase used by one of the organizers to justify his rejection of my participation only serves to confirm my theory about the aims of many of these training events: *"We're not going to just let you go out there and shoot us in the foot"*.

D. Google searches.

As you already know, Google is the most well known, most frequently used search engine in the world. That's why the 4th step in my research was to exploit Mr. Google to ensure I was leaving no stone unturned.

With time to spend, and knowing where and how to search, Google can provide you with various strategies, tricks and tools which will help you manage your brand in a much more efficient way.

If that wasn't enough, in my particular case Google proved to be not only an excellent means of discovering tricks and tools which would never make it through the selection process at branding events or a publishing company's strict criteria, but also helped me to discover that (thanks to Google Alerts) a group of designers and programmers were getting organized to, and I quote, "FIND AND LYNCH ME".

Turns out that, as I've already said, **not everyone is happy about me spilling the secrets that I'm sharing in this book.**

1.3. What is branding.

Besides delving into the various tools and strategies to create your own brand, it is essential to define what branding means and explain some basic concepts which tend to cause confusion.

Traditionally, particularly in SMEs, branding has been strictly relegated to a design function, such as, for example, creating a logo.

This is a simplistic and incorrect approach, because any activity carried out by the company is liable to influence our customers' perception of the brand.

Branding is the discipline concerned with creating and managing a brand, and is made up of:

- **Identity** (corporate): Who we are.
- **Image** (corporate): Who our clients say we are.

I realize that sometimes it can be difficult to differentiate between these two concepts, in particular if you haven't read anything about branding before.

Although I get approached on a daily basis by clients who want to work on their or their company's brand, I've come to realize that very few are able to even distinguish between the brand's image and identity. This is obviously not due to a lack of access to information, given that there are 100s of books and articles whose aim is to clarify these two concepts – with no apparent success.

The confusion arises from the fact that outside of the world of branding, these terms are used in a different way. Thus, according to the Collins English Dictionary:

- The **image** of a person, group, or organization is the way that they appear to other people.
- The **identity** of a person or place is the characteristics they have that distinguish them from others.

Corporate image is the generally held perception of a brand (what our clients say about us) and as such, is not always something we can control. However, we can create and manage our corporate identity as we deem fit via proper brand management. So, identity is what we will learn to build efficiently in this book.

Corporate identity is in turn made up of:

- **Brand identity**: Who you are inside.
- **Formal identity**: How you present yourself to the world.

This naming convention can vary depending on which author you're reading, but the important thing is to understand and distinguish between the meaning of the two concepts.

1.3.1. Your professional stylist.

In order to try and clarify these two concepts, I'm going to draw on what I learned when I was working shoulder to shoulder with a professional stylist on the production of a well-known clothing brand's catalog. This is the example I like to use with my clients and it has always done the trick. It's also a really useful way of introducing and underlining the concept of target customers.

First off, I want you to imagine that your company/brand is you yourself, and your target customer is that person you've got the hots for.

The importance of having a clearly identified target customer.

If you go through life trying to find a partner but you've never stopped to think what that special person should be like, there's a high chance you're either going to spend the rest of your life with the wrong person, never find anyone because you're looking in the wrong places, or even not notice when the perfect match is standing right in front of you.

I'm not talking about being obsessed with one single person. What I mean is that you should have a clear idea of what that person should be like, what requirements the type of person you'd like to attract and to be with should fulfill. I recommend you spend some time coming up with a list of things you're looking for in a partner: physical qualities, personality, values, hobbies etc. The more detailed the list, the better.

When it comes down to it, if you haven't prepared your list in advance, then you run the risk of falling for the first person to say they like you following an extended period on your lonesome ownsome.

What is more, without a clear idea of the type of person you want to share your life with, how do you know where to find them, or what you can do to attract them and make them fall in love with you?

It's the same when it comes to target clients. If you don't spend the necessary time on identifying them inside out – how they think, what interests them, where they spend time, etc. – the how the hell are you ever going to find them?

The importance of consistency between our brand identity and our formal identity.

Let's imagine that once you have identified your ideal partner (**target client**), you decide that the best way to attract their attention and get them to notice you is with your choice of outfits (**formal identity**). Given that you presumably don't want to leave this chance of love in the hands of fate, you decide to take control and hire a professional stylist who can advise you on the best way of dressing to entice the guy or gal of your dreams.

If you've found yourself a genuinely good stylist, then before getting down to business, they will ask you not only about the type of person you want to attract and the occasion you're dressing up for, but also questions about you: what are you like, what are you interested in, etc. (**brand identity**). In this way, rather than dressing you up as someone that's just not you, they can help you to make the most of yourself through your outfits and accessories that best match your personal style.

If you're only looking for a one night stand, then dressing up as someone you're not might work (**advertising**), but if you want a relationship that stands the test of time, the best strategy is to harness your own style, enhancing and conveying the best facets of your personality (**branding**).

Therefore, before seeking professional guidance on your wardrobe, you should first of all know yourself deep down – because a good stylist will help you choose your outfits (**formal identity**) based on the person you want to attract (**target client**) and the occasion you're dressing up for, but all within the framework of who *you* really are (**brand identity**).

Branding is not about dressing ourselves up to be more attractive to clients. Rather, it's about choosing the outfit that best conveys who we are, so that those clients can easily pick us out from the crowd.

1.4. Why you should use branding.

Over the last three decades, brands have gone from being just one more asset that makes up a business, to being the key asset. A brand is the fundamental component in a company's survival due to both its ability to generate income and its inherent financial value. Thus, the brand asset is one of the business' most important, and its strategic management becomes a necessity for all businesses.

In this context, any enterprise, regardless of its turnover and number of staff, should pay attention to its branding strategy and afford it the weight it deserves.

The aim of branding it to create brand equity, or in other words, brand value. This brand value is twofold: brand value for the consumer and brand value for the company. The realization of brand value for the consumer, achieved by connecting the customer both rationally and emotionally with the brand, will in turn lead to brand value for the company.

1.4.1. Strategic advantages of branding.

A. Strategic management tool.

"A positive corporate image is a condition for continuity and strategic success. It is no longer solely the field of attention of marketing, but a strategic instrument of top management" (De Soet, in Blaw, 1994).

B. Boost for the product, labor and financial markets.

A solid corporate image is a boost for the sale of products and services.

"It helps the company to recruit the best employees, is important for financial operators and investors, and builds trust between internal and external target audiences" (Blaw, 1994).

In this way, a powerful brand image means the services and/or products you offer will be the ones chosen by the target client, and the business itself will be chosen by employees and staff.

C. Added value and the competitive factor.

A solid corporate image creates added emotional value for a company, and ensures it stays one step ahead of the game.

"A solid corporate image is competitive, in other words, distinct and credible" (Brinckerhoff, 1990).

To set yourself apart from your competitors and carve out a niche in your field, you need to create a brand image that reflects the added value you bring to the market.

D. Attracting different audiences.

"A good image helps a business to attract the people necessary for its success: analysts, investors, clients, partners and staff. Identity management guarantees this good image" (Chajet, 1989).

A business with a well-honed brand image attracts and generates great interest compared to those that don't spend time on it or do so insufficiently.

E. Differentiation factor.

"Various studies have shown that 9 out of 10 consumers state that, when it comes to choosing between products that are similar in terms of price and quality, the company's reputation determines which product or service they will purchase," (Mackiewicz, 1993).

If you don't work on your branding from the get-go, you will be missing out on opportunities when it comes to competing with others who offer similar products and/or services.

F. It facilitates decision-making.

It does so when:

- The information with which to make decisions is complex, conflicting, and/or incomplete.
- The information is insufficient or covers too much to be able to make a judgment.
- "There are certain conditions in the environment that obstruct the decision making process, such as a lack of time" (Poiesz, 1988).

1.4.2. Specific advantages for each business area.

These broad, strategic advantages can crystallize into specific advantages for each business area:

A. Internal level of business.

- Branding increases motivation among all members of staff in a company.
- It is an important factor in attracting staff, partners, and investors.
- It improves the final quality of the products and/or services offered.

B. Marketing and Promotion Level.

- It boosts the client's perception of the quality of products and/or services.
- It fosters and accelerates the decision making process of potential clients.
- It increases customer loyalty and encourages peer recommendations.

Summary of the major benefits of branding for your business.

- It helps you to stand out from your competitors.
- It allows you to pick and create a strong identity for your products and/or services.
- It generates prestige, credibility and confidence, so vital to the purchasing decisions of your potential client.

1.5. Why branding isn't used.

Now that we've seen the various advantages that stem from good brand management, it seems obvious that any entrepreneurs or businessmen who *aren't* doing everything within their power – or worse, are doing nothing at all – to build or improve their brand must simply not be aware of the benefits. However, over the course of my research and analysis of the businesses within my vicinity, I have discovered that there are many business people who *are* aware of the advantages outlined above.

So, if they do realize how important such strategies are, why on earth are they not harnessing their brands?

The reasons I uncovered were broadly twofold:

Reason #1: They see it as an expensive thing to do.

In general, many people hold the erroneous belief that creating a brand is super expensive and only something big businesses can afford to do. This is a fairly widespread belief among businesses, business people, and small business managers.

I didn't have to go too far to find examples of companies that thought branding was too expensive for them.

Although I currently live in the States, I was born and raised in Elda, a small Spanish town just twenty short minutes' drive from the Mediterranean and known internationally for its footwear industry, its main economic activity.

The town has lived through periods of splendor in which everyone, both business owners and workers, experienced very high standards of living. Sadly, this wealth was based purely on the old adage of being "in the right place at the right time". The business owners themselves started out as workers – enterprising ones for sure, but without any formal business training – who set up small workshops which, spurred by the economic bonanza, ended up becoming huge business empires managed by these very people, and their children after them. They believed that everything they had achieved was fruit of their hard work.... and just sat back and relaxed.

Unfortunately for these business owners and their workers, the economic crisis combined with globalization woke them out of their very own little fairy tale. Thus during the period from 2000 to 2015, 95% of the companies shut down, while those that managed to survive became slaves to major international brands that pay third-world salaries to manufacture luxury shoes that they then sell at exorbitant prices.

It comes as no surprise that someone who has studied Business Studies can predict, without any prior knowledge of the footwear industry, that if a company doesn't work on its branding, sooner or later it will end up being absorbed by one that does, even if that other company has no clue about footwear.

What surprised me was to discover that many of these business owners who had to fold their companies or were struggling every month just to keep afloat and pay their staff, were also aware of this fact.

I remember that some time ago in a conversation with my father, who began working in footwear at the age of 13 and who, during the 10 years prior to his retirement worked for some 7 different companies (always as a result of the previous one's closure), he explained to me that his boss had argued with the representative of a major brand because it was threatening to move production to another country (China, if my memory is correct) if he didn't lower his prices even further. Specifically, this rep was looking to pay $20 per finished shoe instead of $23, the sum he was paying at that point. It may not seem like a big difference but if you figure in that at $23 per shoe, a worker was making just $3 per hour and that the shoes themselves would be sold to the public for somewhere between $600 and $900, then the boss' ire was more than justified. Anyhow, he ultimately had to submit to the demands.

After hearing this story, which was sadly all-too-familiar, I explained to my father that if his boss had dedicated time to creating his own brand it would be he who could choose the price at which to sell his shoes, and he wouldn't have to accept abusive, externally imposed prices. Naively, I thought I was giving a little lesson in branding to my father, but as I said, I was surprised at how aware my father already was of all this, and even more surprised to know that his boss was just as aware.

I asked then why the boss hadn't done anything about it, to which he replied that he couldn't afford it, creating a brand was too costly.

Couldn't afford it? The truth was that he "couldn't af-
ford" not to, and continue to accept prices for his shoes
that didn't even cover the cost of production.

– Why do you think it's so expensive? – I asked.

He explained that an old boss of his, long before the
crisis began, was on the verge of bankruptcy thanks to trying to set up her own brand, despite cutting expenditure as
much as possible.

So, what exactly was the "low cost" branding strategy of
this businesswoman?

1. Use your daughter instead of hiring a professional
   model. Savings of $50-100 per session. This is NOT
   low cost branding.
2. Take advantage of one of your nephews "being good
   at" photography rather than hiring a professional
   photographer. Savings of $100-200 per session.
   This is NOT low cost branding.
3. Publish the resulting photos in the best national
   and international fashion magazines. Investment:
   between $3,000 and $12,000 per publication per
   month. THIS IS NOT LOW COST BRANDING!

Reason #2: Lack of knowledge and/or fear.

We don't know exactly what it's all about, or it might sound like witchcraft to our ears, this branding stuff. And we all fear the unknown.

In my family, besides my parents, everyone either is or was a business person. However as with many business owners, they have never developed their brands nor have any intention of doing so. Some of my relatives work on the production of exceptional products, with no competitors, while others provide more common services but in an equally exceptional way.

While both types of business benefit hugely from a minor investment in branding – some to advertise their business and sell on a global scale, and others to position themselves as a benchmark in their sector at a local or provincial level, none of my family members has ever approached me about the subject, even though they've all experienced economic difficulties or have even considered shutting down *"due to the crisis"*

I, who fully recognize that this branding nonsense sounds like Chinese (whispers) to my family, have never attempted to guide or advise them when it comes to their businesses, sad and regrettable as that fact may be. On one occasion however, during the course of a conversation in which one of my relatives was telling me about how much it was costing him to keep his business afloat in spite of the exceptional service they provided and the major investment they had just made in the best machinery the industry could offer, it occurred to me, naively, to offer to prepare a market research report and develop a website with a clearly defined positioning strategy, with the aim of acquiring new customers and allowing the business to play with its profit margins a little. All for free. His answer epitomizes many business owners' way of thinking. I'm quoting word for word here, as it remains etched on my brain:

"Hey, don't get me mixed up in one of your scams, we're family!"

I responded with a feeble *"OK"*, took a deep breath, telling myself not to take it personally, then left.

We've never spoken about the subject again.

Did this response mean he didn't really care much about his company, or that he didn't trust me? No. In many businesses, particularly those that are handed down from parents to children, generation after generation, until the market ousts them (this will only become more and more common), the owners end up wrongly believing that if they've made it so far it's because they're doing something right, and because they can't put a finger on what exactly that is, the only way to keep doing so is not to change a thing:

- "It works just fine as it is."
- "It would never work for us."
- "We are not prepared for that."
- "We'll leave it for now."
- "Now is not the best time."
- "We're going to wait for things to get better."
- Etc.

People fear the new, the unknown, and the consequences of this can turn out to be extremely expensive.

Shutting your company down is nothing compared to everything you can lose over the course of a lifetime, both personally and professionally, thanks to that irrational fear of change.

1.6. Why you shouldn't put it off.

I'm sure that if you're reading this book then you're already well aware of the importance of branding, and have decided to harness it for your company or project, meaning I don't need to go on and on about its benefits in an attempt to convince you.

What you may need some convincing of is to start as soon as possible. Whether you're only just thinking about launching your project, or have been on the market for some time already, I'd like to give you two good reasons to stop putting the decision off.

1. You'll reach break-even sooner.

If you haven't yet launched your project or you're in the first stages of development, working on branding RIGHT NOW will help you to generate profit sooner.

But why?!

Given that most business people and entrepreneurs delay the decision to work on their brand until things are "going well"[1], when we stumble across a company with an established brand, we automatically presume that things must already be going well, or great, and we subconsciously ascribe these good results to a series of features common to all successful businesses: safety, quality, professionalism, etc.

Hence, by establishing your brand from the get-go, you're taking advantage of that subconscious association that is sparked in the minds of your potential clients, who will ascribe the same set of characteristics to *your* company as they do to others that have struggled for years to reach the same level of recognition. And that, of course, translates into increased sales.

Example:

On one occasion, a businessman from the footwear sector got in touch with me, as he had invested a considerable sum of money in producing a small range

---

[1] *Unfortunately, putting off this decision means in many cases, that things never go well, or in the best case scenario, take much longer to produce positive results.*

of high end ladies' footwear, but had neglected to consider how he was going to sell them once made, competing with other well established brands on the market at the same price point.

The strategy followed: create an online shop with stronger branding than your direct competitors: name, logo, website, photography, etc.

Marketing investment: $0

Result: in under one month he had sold all of his stock, ordered the production of the next batch, and increased prices by 30% All via the internet and without the need for an intermediary.

Why: establishing a visual identity from the very start, mimicking and improving it in comparison with its competitors, allows you to harness the positive associations that such brands have spent years building up in their clients' minds, as well as to remove the trepidation that comes with purchasing a new brand on a hitherto unfamiliar website.

2. It allows you to grow your profits.

If your business has been up and running for some time and you're simply looking to give it a boost and improve profitability, now is the time to work on branding.

The simple act of defining the type of customer you want to target, or of improving your visual identity, can help you grow your revenue overnight.

Furthermore, any other actions or strategies carried out at your company will be far more profitable if you have already established the brand.

Example:

> At the start of 2015 a team of entrepreneurs that had set up a marketing agency asked me for help, as they were already losing their will to work and thinking about shutting down and moving on.
>
> The problem was that three years previously, when they opened their marketing agency, they started out by offering their services at a cut-price rate. As they told me, they decided to set these prices as it made them feel good to think that this strategy would help other entre-

preneurs such as themselves to forge ahead with their own projects.

However, it didn't take long for them to realize that the type of client they were receiving didn't appreciate their work at all, complained about absolutely everything and before long, would cancel all services contracted, arguing that they were too expensive.

Solution: define the type of client they wanted to work with, design a new visual identity in keeping with their new objectives/clients and... increase prices five-fold.

Result: although their prices had increased, in less than 3 months we managed to double the company's revenue, reduce the workload by half and work with more serious clients, ones who were more qualified and valued the work more.

Why: prices that were too low[2] and a visual identity that was somewhat childish and dated had created distrust and rejection in exactly the type of client they hoped to attract.

---

[2] *To give you a better idea of just how low the prices were, I can tell you that even when we increased them five-fold they were still way below the market average.*

1.7. DIY: Do it yourself or outsource.

Does establishing a brand on a limited budget mean that you have to learn how to do everything for yourself?

Absolutely NOT, in fact it's pretty much the opposite. As far as possible I recommend you delegate different branding tasks to the most appropriate professional in each case.

How can you know when it's best to delegate and when it's more appropriate to do things for yourself?

Below you will find a detailed list of requirements that will help you determine whether or not it's a good idea to delegate or outsource tasks related to your business. It should prove useful for matters related to branding as well as any other area of your business.

If you can't move past any of these points, then arguably the best thing to do is delegate.

Let's take a look!

A. Can you do it to as good as standard, or better, as a professional would?

This is the most important point, because the idea is not to do something "adequate" on a low budget, but to achieve *professional results* on a low budget. If you aren't able to do something to the same standard as a professional, then do not hesitate to outsource.

But how can you tell if you're able to complete a task to the same quality as a good professional would? Well, ask yourself these questions:

- Could I make a living out of it, as a professional?
- If my prices were the same, would a client contract me?

B. Do your sums: Are you really going to save money?

Let's imagine that alongside your entrepreneurial passion, you're an artist in your free time, or you've taken a community management course, or your hobbies are photography and videography. Does that make it easier for you undertake those aspects of branding by yourself? NO.

I recommend you do something really simple, something we don't normally do when we're determined to save money. Gather various quotes for the task in question, and choose the one you're happiest with (going on gut feeling, trust, professionalism, recommendations, etc.). Now do the following: calculate how long it would take you to do the same task, multiply that sum by two (and that's too little, we don't realize how far we underestimate the time it takes for such tasks) then multiply the result by your hourly fee. If the final sum (in dollars) is less than the quote you've chosen, then go to the next point. If not, outsource.

C. Do you want to take on the job?

It's crucial to ask yourself this question.

Because no matter how much you save, or how well you can do the task in question, surely your business or the project you'd like to launch already takes up 100% of your time, without need for additional branding tasks on top? So if said task is not something that – apart from saving you time – you actually want to do, even in your free time, then I thoroughly recommend delegating and allowing yourself to concentrate on running the business.

D. Do you really have time to do it?

Sometimes, no matter how good our skills and knowledge of a particular task may be, no matter how much you might save, or how much you really want to do the task at hand yourself, time is what it is, and there are only so many hours in a day. When you're running your own business, whether large or small, you should be aware that you can't do everything by yourself, and at some point you'll have to delegate certain tasks to be able to focus on other more important ones.

Now you're armed with the information necessary to decide exactly which tasks to take on yourself and which to outsource to the professionals.

CHAPTER ONE

Brand identity

First things first, before choosing a cool name, or rushing to design your own logo, or setting up your own website (**formal identity**), as a brand you should be clear about who you are, what you want to achieve, what you believe in, and what niche you want to fill both in the market and the minds of your potential customers (**brand identity**). To successfully build your brand, this needs to be reflected in the mission, vision and values of your company, and you should be aware of how to position it intelligently vis-à-vis your competitors.

It is crucial to take sufficient time to develop these strategic principles in advance, as a large part of your future success will depend on them. Don't make the mistake of leaving this stage until later, choosing instead to focus on tasks that seem more agreeable.

Defining these criteria from the start will save you both time and money.

Don't be fooled by the percentage of this book dedicated to brand identity compared to formal identity, because beyond a shadow of a doubt, the former is the factor with the greatest potential to catapult your brand the highest.

This may seem a difficult undertaking and, due to its importance, something that should be left to the professionals, but in the last chapter where we discussed a series of tasks that are better done by you yourself, this is exactly what I was talking about. There is NO-ONE better placed to develop these principles than the business owner him or herself. Nobody knows your business or project better than you. All you need is someone to guide you, and that's what I, my friend, am here for. I'm going to make the whole process smoother and more enjoyable. By simply answering a series of questions, you will – without realizing it – have established your strategic principles better than any branding agency could have done for you.

Let's get to work!

2.1. Mission.

Whether you took Business Studies or not, I'm sure the term "mission" (in a business context) sounds rather abstract, and you're probably not sure exactly what its connection to branding is, or how it can be beneficial when it comes to building your brand.

There are many ways to define a company's mission. Here's one I really like:

The mission is your company's purpose beyond making money.

Your mission should allude to your company's raison d'être, its very essence, why it exists in the first place.

A well-formulated and clearly communicated purpose is one of the most powerful tools to convince customers to choose your brand over others. In this section you will learn how to create an inspiring mission statement that makes you stand out from the crowd. And best of all, you'll do it for completely free.

2.1.1. How to create your mission.

If you've never thought about it before, then a good place to start is by answering this question:

What is the purpose of your company beyond making money?

The idea behind answering this question is to connect emotionally with your clients. Now is not the time to explain the features of your product or services but to create a rapport with your clients on a deeper level, because ultimately, emotions are what drive us to choose specific products over others.

Of course, when you decide to set up a business, one of your aims is to make money – after all, there are bills to be paid, mortgages, staff salaries, suppliers, etc. But your company, over and above its economic aims, should also address a deeper purpose for you, your clients, and the world in general. Therefore, when it comes to creating your mission, keep in mind how your purpose works from these three perspectives.

2.1.2. Brainstorming.

A. Your reasons:

- What inspired you to undertake this project?
- Why do you do what you do?
- How will this project help you to achieve your dreams?
- What pushed you to set up your own business?

B. Your clients' reasons:

- What problems/needs do your clients have?
- How can your company help them to solve these problems?
- What emotional needs does it address for your clients? Do you inspire them to achieve their dreams? Do you help them overcome their fears?
- How do your products/services help to improve your clients' lives?

C. The world's reasons:

- How is your business going to improve the world?
- How does your business help people's general well-being?

- How does your business look after the environment?

Great, once you've answered these questions you can begin to compose your mission, the reason why your clients should become your unconditional followers, the reason that drives you to jump out of bed in the mornings, an inspiring mission that makes people choose your products instead of your competitors'.

Now it's time to gather these three perspectives together: look for the underlying theme in all of your answers. In your mission, try to communicate the thing that connects *your* reasons with those of your clients, and the world.

Note*: Your company's mission should summarize what you do, who you do it for, and how you do it.*

2.2. Vision.

Now that you've worked out your purpose as a company it will prove much easier to define the vision that will guide you and keep you on the right track towards the achievement of your aims and objectives.

A vision defines and describes the future situation that the company wishes to be in.

Try to answer these questions:

- What do you want your company to be like in the next few years?
- Where is your company headed?
- What do you wish to achieve as a business?
- Where do you see the business five years from now?

Look at your vision as a route map which sets out your goals in both the medium and long term. It will act as a compass and let you make the necessary changes of direction if you get lost on route towards said goals.

Your vision should be motivating, and therefore realistic and achievable.

But how does all this add value for your clients? Do they really care where you're headed, or where you want to get to?

2.2.1. Why will your vision make you stand out from the crowd?

The majority of businesses fail when it comes to creating their company vision because they forget about their customers' interests and motivations. Your company's vision should serve you as a strategic map in the long term, but if you want it to also work as a tool for the acquisition and retention of customers, then don't forget about them when composing it.

As you saw in the previous point, it is critical to connect with your customers on an emotional level. Only when your vision is able to inspire and motivate your clients, as well as you, will you be able to differentiate yourself and stand out from 99% of the competition.

To create your company vision, let's do a little visualization exercise. I want you to close your eyes and imagine yourself in 5 to 10 years time, having achieved the objectives that, right now, seem so far away.

2.2.2. Brainstorming.

- How do you feel?
- Where are you?
- What do you do all day?
- What have you taught your clients?
- How have you changed the lives of your clients?
- What's it like working on your team?
- What does the media say about your company?
- How have you impacted the sector you work in?
- How has your company contributed to creating a better world?

Once you've come up with a few ideas about how you envisage the future, you need to think about how you will measure your progress and achievements until you realize it. It's important to be as detailed as possible, ensuring that you know beyond a shadow of a doubt that you have achieved what you set out to do.

One of the best ways of composing your vision is to define both your objective and how you will measure its achievement. On writing down your vision, don't forget to keep your clients at the forefront of your ideas. This means that your vision should describe how your products or services will have a positive impact on your clients' lives.

2.2.3. Tips for composing your company vision.

- It should be achievable, not a fantasy.
- It should be inspiring and motivating for both you and your clients.
- It should be clear and simple. Easy to communicate.

2.3. Values.

Have you ever dreamed about hiring another "you" for the team? Have you ever asked yourself how you can ensure that the people you do hire behave the way you want them to? Would you like suppliers, partners and staff to fully understand your way of seeing and doing things?

The answer is to be very clear about what you hold important and what you value. The correct establishment and communication of your brand values is the best way to inject your DNA into the business.

If you plan to work with a team of people, have a partner or hire employees, you need to be clear about what is important *to you.*

This is also important when outsourcing certain business duties or tasks.

Delegating with more peace of mind that things will be done as you hope is possible when you have first established your brand's values.

These values can be tremendously powerful if you can keep them alive within your company's culture, as they define how you want people to act, they set the standards that staff are hired and fired on, they attract employees and customers who identify with your brand, etc. But in order for your values to fulfill their mandate, they must reflect reality, i.e. they must be honest.

It's not enough to just compose a few values based on the fact they "sound good", or "sell more".

Values represent the way you act, even when there's nobody watching.

Nowadays it seems that the corporate values of so many companies are exactly the same. It doesn't matter whether it's a firm making space craft, a political party, or a company selling soda – integrity, excellence or commitment are the values that are bandied about time and again, losing impact each time you hear them.

Customers aren't stupid, we no longer believe everything we read or everything that is said about a certain product or service. We're tired of default values and generic phrases whose only redeeming feature is sounding good. Internet and social media have finally allowed us to discover the truth hidden behind the wall many businesses build to screen themselves from reality. In the olden days a slogan was enough to get us firmly in their pockets; now we need much more. The power that businesses have to disguise reality and manipulate perceptions, with the goal of making us buy their products and services, is becoming smaller by the day.

Your values shouldn't describe what you want or are trying to be, but what you in fact are.

It's time to tell the truth!

Unless you are a "big brand" with a million dollar bank account you can use to whitewash your image every time you get caught doing the opposite of what you said, in other words, your supposed values, then I recommend that you avoid promising things you can't follow through on.

The time has come when, in order to know what a brand is lacking, we just have to take a look at its values. This is one of the best examples of "show me what you're boasting about and I'll tell you what you're lacking". Sad but true. Don't fall in the trap.

Thus, we find the major political powers bragging about and monopolizing their discourse with messages of transparency while practicing strategies of total opacity, or we see large businesses such as Zara positioning values such as "professional ethics" at the top of their values pyramid, all while being sanctioned for slavery.

Example:

> A few years ago I attended a conference on branding given by Luis Chico de Guzmán, CEO of the well-known footwear brand Hispanitas, during he spent over 2 hours expounding the importance of transmitting his brand values (happiness) to every level, from his employees to the end consumer, then ended by admitting, in the question and answer session, that the truth was very different, that they were only interested in selling and had sadly forgotten about people.

What brand values are and are NOT

- Our values have been with us since childhood, they're not a trend.
- The values represent our actions, NOT our desires or goals.
- The values reveal who we are, NOT who we want to be.
- Our values are present when people are watching and when they're NOT.

On this basis, let's perform a small self-analysis to identify your true values, and set them apart from the behavior you aspire to.

2.3.1. Brainstorming.

A. What bugs you?

Discovering your true values requires knowing yourself deep down and being aware of exactly what you can't stand. Recognizing what you don't like or what you disagree with can greatly help you to define your values, as the opposite will be exactly what you *do* value. For example, let's say you can't stand lies no matter how small, not even white lies or fibs – you can thus deduce that one of your values is honesty.

B. What can your childhood tell you about your values?

I'll ask you to think back to your childhood, because that's where your values were forged. During childhood you were educated according to certain standards and these progressively shaped your current values. Who you were, what you cherished, what you disagreed with and how you behaved when you were a child say a lot about your true values.

C. When you are the customer, how do you like to be treated?

Bring to mind your own experiences as a customer, both good and bad. What have been your worst customer experiences? Which exceeded your expectations? Do you like having a certain level of autonomy as a customer, or do you prefer not to have to worry about a thing? As a consumer, what do you value about the customer service of other brands?

D. What do your actions say about your values?

Our actions unveil everything about our true values. How do you compete in life and in business? What type of food do you eat? How do you choose a partner? Every one of your actions, no matter how small, speaks volumes about your values. Can you find a common thread?

E. How would you define success?

If your main aim is to make money, that will affect how you make decisions, how you measure the performance of your staff, etc. The opposite extreme would be a person who, above all, wishes to create a positive impact on people and the world at large. What does your definition of success say about your values? Who do you see as successful people? What do you take into account in your definition? At what point do you regard yourself as having achieved success? What factors are you weighing up in your considerations?

2.3.2. How can you compose your brand values?

Once you have thoroughly explored what it is you truly value, it's time to compose your brand values. The easier they are to remember, the better.

Let's take a look at how to write your corporate values in 2 simple steps, in a way that will connect with your clients, staff, partners, consumers, etc.:

1. Keep it simple. Choose 3-5 values that are easy to remember.
2. Make it memorable: write your values as slogans.

Example:

The best example that springs to mind is that of Royal Caribbean, a company I worked for when I was just 20 and whose slogan I remember to this day: *"Deliver the Wow"*. This awesome slogan also happened to be 100% reality, with all of the employees sticking to that one simple guideline, endeavoring to amaze our customers by exceeding their expectations in each and every one of our interactions with them.

So don't take the crafting of your values lightly, confining yourself to copying those that feature in 99% of businesses. If you devote sufficient time to reflect, and keep in mind everything I've outlined in this section, you'll find that your values create huge added value which will be recognized and appreciated by your clientele.

These values will serve as a code of conduct for you and your employees when performing any business task. Furthermore, together with your vision, they will serve as a route map when you experience tough times.

2.4. Positioning.

A brand's position is the niche it fills, or aspires to fill, in the consumer's mind.

This should not be confused with "web positioning" or "SEO positioning", which is the ranking of a website on internet search engines (e.g. Google).

2.4.1. Why is positioning the most important decision that you'll have to make?

Brand positioning is the most important decision, as well as the most complicated one, that the entrepreneur has to make. How bold you are when it comes to positioning your brand on the market will determine in large part the future success of your business.

Positioning defines why customers should choose you and not your rivals.

In this section you will identify what type of client you're hoping to attract and what makes your product or service unique in order to define your brand's positioning.

When a customer asks me to create a website for their business, create their visual identity or manage some of their social networks, and I ask them "what makes you different or unique?", the answers tend to be strikingly similar: "we offer quality products", "we are the best in our field", "we've been in this business for X number of years", "we are unique", etc.

As one of the speakers at a marketing conference I attended a few years ago so eloquently explained, when someone used stock phrases such as these to describe why their product or service was unique, his reply would be *"Great, what else?"*.

The thing is that, as with company values, it seems every company is using the same messages over and over, which lose their significance and powers of persuasion, becoming invisible to the eyes of potential customers.

You need to be much, much more specific when it comes to defining your positioning and conveying what makes you unique.

It's time to be bold.

Well defined positioning not only requires you to decide what type of consumer you want to reach, but also what type you DON'T want to reach. This means that the more specific you are, the more consumers you will rule out of your target audience. And that requires a lot of courage.

When we set up a business, we tend to think that the more numerous and varied the type of client to which we can offer our products or services, the more possibilities we will have of acquiring clients.

The fact of the matter is that, **when everybody is your customer, nobody is**.

You cannot and should not be everything to everyone.

The more specialized your products and services are, the more possibilities you have of becoming an effective solution to addressing the needs of your potential customers.

Focusing on the customers you want to reach allows you to focus your energy where it needs to be rather than competing with others who do the same as you. Don't feel bad about excluding a certain type of client. Sometimes we have to say "no" to create enough space to say "yes".

When you're settling on your market niche (the group of people your product portfolio is aimed at), this should seem ridiculously small to you. If your definition of target consumers is "people between the ages of 20 and 40", then you need to go back to the drawing board and narrow it down.

Try to put a face to your ideal client. Keep that in mind and try to answer questions such as: "How old are they?", "Is it a man or a woman?", "What is their purchasing power?", "What motivates them in life?", "What do they hate?", "What does they worry about?", "How do they dress?", "What magazines do they read?", "What brands do they use?", "What celebrities or influencers do they follow?", "What motivates them to buy a certain product?", "How do they behave online?", "What social networks, forums and platforms do they use?".

This simple exercise will give you plenty of ideas that enable you to define your brand positioning, as well as providing valuable information to help you know where to find your target client and how to attract them too, ensuring they're buying what you're selling.

2.4.2. How can you create your brand positioning?

Now let's explore what you want to be known for, and determine the type of reputation you'd like to build around your brand. It's vital that you're honest here. It is essential that you feel passionate about and comfortable with the type of client you are going to sell to. Thus it shouldn't be a decision you make lightly, based on no more than the potential profits from your chosen market sector.

The ultimate aim of defining your positioning is to be able to stop competing with your rivals. You need to be unique. The first step to positioning your brand is to determine *who* you are selling to or want to sell to, and *what* you are selling.

2.4.3. Brainstorming.

A. Who are you selling to?

- Who would buy your product or service?
- Men or women?
- How old are they?
- What is their lifestyle like?
- Where do they live?
- Etc.

The more questions you ask yourself, the clearer your vision of the target customer will be.

It helps tremendously to put a name to the face of your ideal customer, and keep them in mind – always.

It is possible that you are targeting two different customer profiles, in which case, complete the exercise for each one separately.

B. What are you selling?

- In what industry or sector are you competing?
- What is your area of expertise?
- What type of products and/or services do you offer?

C. What is your "value proposition"?

- What will drive consumers to choose your products and/or services over your competitors'?
- What is there that only you can contribute? What do you do better than anyone else?
- What results do you bring to your potential client that others do not?

- What do you do differently and uniquely to achieve that result?

Once you've answered these questions you can pinpoint your positioning in a single sentence.

2.4.4. How will you know if you've gone for the right positioning?

- Your competitors would be envious of you if you launched this strategy on the market.
- Your professional colleagues think you're crazy because your niche is too specific.
- None of your competitors are doing the same.
- The clientele outlined is not currently being addressed.
- People will talk about you and your brand because it's different.

Formal Identity

We've come to the stage where you should already have formally set down your mission, vision and brand values, as well as having decided what position you want to have on the market.

Now that you know who you are and what you want to achieve, it´s time to work on the way you want to present yourself to the world, your brand´s formal identity. This can be split into:

- **Verbal identity**: name, slogan, vocabulary, tone of voice, etc.
- **Visual identity**: logo, fonts, corporate colors, etc.

Why do you need to work on your formal identity "regardless of the size of your business"?

Formal identity is one of the most important aspects of any business because this is how the business manages to convey its personality and the features that define and distinguish it to its target audience.

Let's do a little experiment. I'll give you the name of a brand, and you have to think of the first thing about that brand that springs to mind:

- McDonald's
- Apple
- Zara
- Coca-Cola
- BMW

I'm sure the first thing you visualized on reading each brand name was their logo (the symbol representing them). After visualizing the logo, you most likely though about some of the values or slogans you naturally associate with these brands:

- McDonald's: tasty, burgers and chips, fast food, cheap, "I'm loving it"...

- Apple: elitist, expensive, design, style, innovation...
- Zara: cheap, stylish clothes...
- Coca-Cola: happiness, bubbles, joy, cooling down when it's hot...
- BMW: reliability, safe cars, high purchasing power, "Do you like to drive?"...

There are many reasons these things come to mind first. The 2 mains ones are:

1. Strong advertising:

Not only the number of ads that you see for these brands, but also the creation of brilliant slogans that permeate the subconscious: *"Do you like to drive?"*, *"I'm lovin' it!"*...

2. A product that lives up to expectation:

No matter how much marketing you do, if the hamburgers don't taste good, the computers don't perform well, or the BMWs malfunction more often that a fairground rifle, the message will not get through and the consumer will not "internalize" the brand in a positive way.

However, none of this would filter down to you as a consumer if it weren't for these companies having a well-defined formal identity. Specific symbols, slogans, colors, names and fonts, used in the same way wherever the brand may be. Each of these different elements of the brand ensures that its positive values (price, quality... whatever it may be) are associated with its corporate identity.

These **formal elements act as a trigger in your brain**. *You see or hear them, and bam!, all of the connotations flourish in your mind.*

And in spite of its importance, this point is one where small and medium enterprises usually fail to deliver, believing that it's not for them, it's only for the big brands.

Here you can see **3 major reasons** for buckling down and spending the time and effort required to define your formal identity, whatever size your business may be:

1. Scale doesn't matter.

This is first and foremost, and you should have it clear: all social groups function in pretty much the same way.

A multinational will have to look for a way to reach millions of consumers on all five continents, while your company possibly only needs to reach the online public in the US, or even just those in your town or neighborhood. No matter. It comes down to a group of people who don't know you and who, when they do, will place a value on your product or service, and associate it with your brand's image.

The scale this happens on is of little relevance, what counts is that people speak to one another and share their experiences.

A negative brand identity is difficult to escape from.

2. Your audience needs to be able to easily identify and remember you.

To be memorable, both your brand name and your visual identity are crucial.

A good name should be catchy, easy to pronounce. It should sound familiar. Give the feeling that it's always been there.

A carefully chosen logo and a slogan will mean that your audience can remember your brand even if they don't instantly remember your name. And all of this can lead to you increasing the number of clients and in turn, profits.

Furthermore, for many businesses personal recommendations can attract significant numbers of new customers. That's why, if your brand is easy to remember thanks to one of the above, it's far more likely that a satisfied customer will recommend your products and/or services to their friends, acquaintances and family members.

3. You need to minimize your marketing budgets.

Marketing campaigns can be like a black hole in the budget of any company. Not because they're expensive *per se*, but because **investments are often made without any plan or strategy**: *"Now I'm doing SEO for 3 months, now I'm advertising on Facebook, now I'm printing some flyers to see if that works..."*.

The difference between a giant corporation and a small company is simply the amount of money invested, but the issue remains the same: there has to be a strategy.

Starting with a good corporate identity lowers marketing costs in the medium and long term, because:

- All the campaigns you launch are based on the same visual and symbolic foundation, saving time and design costs.
- Spreading the message, when this is launched from the same visual base, expands cumulatively.
- If you have a coherent and positive brand image, the results and effects of any actions executed will be much greater.

A person who, on opening their business, reaches 2,000 consumers with some green flyers, and then another 4,000 on Facebook with a distinctive blue logo designed as an afterthought... has not only wasted their investment on flyers, but will also have to reinvest in reaching those very people once more, with their new image.

A person who reaches 6,000 people from the get-go with a well defined corporate image has not only already arrived, but any subsequent advertising will be a case of "*it never rains but it pours*", swinging the public in their favor.

The aim is that anyone, anywhere, and at any time, can identify your brand and remember it in the same way.

3.1. Verbal Identity.

3.1.1. Naming.

Naming it the term used to refer to the process of choosing, as well as the techniques of creating, a brand name.

With naming, the aim it to ensure that when consumers hear your brand they're able to identify the product, associating it with the features that make it unique.

Its name is the most powerful ambassador a brand can have. It's the business card that consumers commit to memory, their first contact with a brand.

A manufacturing problem, an error in packaging or a failure in the advertising campaign are setbacks that may generate bigger or smaller headaches but which are ultimately rectifiable. However, once a brand name has been launched on the market, there's no going back.

In certain sectors, laziness, haste, a lack of strategy, resources or set criteria are rife. Fortunately, plenty have realized just how important a brand name is, and they are the ones that prove successful.

Settling on the "perfect name" can't be left to chance, rather, it forms part of an increasingly professionalized practice.

Using your brand name as a business strategy is fundamental.

However, you may have heard it said on more than one occasion that the name itself isn't so important. The fact is that there is a group of branding experts or "gurus" who, most probably in an attempt to sell more books and/or stroke their own egos for being able to defend the indefensible, claim that naming is of little importance.

Interview with Jacob Benbunan (a well-known branding guru):

"Naming isn't important at all, I want to set that straight. Any name will do. And if anyone wants to dispute that then they need to explain how, if a name should be something different, distinguished, then companies such as General Electric or American Airlines exist. If someone says that a name needs to be short, then tell them to come here and explain to me how PriceWaterhouseCoopers manages to exist.

If someone tries to say that a name has to be easy to write and to pronounce, then please explain what's going on with Haagen Dazs, with Schweppes. If someone says that a brand name can't have negative connotations, then what about Rabobank (which in Spanish more or less means "*Prickbank*") or Virgin Atlantic... these are all powerful brands."

Well, Jacob is correct... partially. As it turns out, each of these brands have something in common: plenty of time and, above all, plenty of money. If, like these companies, you can also afford to rectify any slip-ups, gaffes or inadequacies by simply flashing the cash, then no, naming is not important. Neither naming nor anything else for than matter. But here we're dealing with the fact you don't want to be "firefighting" with your hard-won earnings, or even worse, with those of other people. So, choose a good name – EXTRA IMPORTANT when you're on a limited budget.

How to come up with your brand name.

Now it's time to stretch your imagination. Based on the following models of syntactic construction make a list of everything that comes to mind. EVERYTHING:

- **Descriptive brand names** are those that readily convey the service or product offered by a company (Bank of America).

- **Evocative brand names** use suggestion and metaphor to bring to mind the experience or positioning of a brand (Nike).

- **Invented brand names** are etymological fabrications that are nothing if not distinctive (Pixar).

- **Lexical brand names** rely on wordplay for their memorability (Dunkin' Donuts).

- **Acronym brand names** (BMW).

- **Geographical brand names** imbue a brand with all the cultural and historical associations of its namesake (American Airlines).

- **Founder brand names** (Ford).

Have you thought of too many names now? Not to worry – choose around 10-20 of your favorites and filter them through the following list of considerations. Consider yourself lucky if more than one makes it out the other end:

Factors to consider when choosing your brand name.

A. Differentiation from competitors.

If your brand name lets you stand out from the crowd of rivals from the outset, that's a good start. Clearly that won't exempt you from keeping up the hard work, but no-one is immune to a little boost, especially at the start. If you want to convey that you're not just another one of many, logic says you need to start differentiating yourself with the very name of your brand.

B. Easy to write and say.

Research confirms that a simple name is the best option.

In psychology, *cognitive fluency* measures how easy it is to think of something. Psychologists have discovered that campaigns conducted by companies with easy-to-pronounce names significantly outperform those with hard-to-pronounce names.

Given that cognitive fluency can affect the way consumers spend their money, branding agencies often recommend avoiding:

- Initials.

- Words in a language different to that of the target market.
- Words that can be pronounced in different ways.
- Words that are difficult to pronounce.

C. International usage.

Think big. If your project manages to transcend national boundaries then you, and it, need to be prepared. A name that sounds good in English doesn't necessarily sound good in other languages. Meanwhile, a name with no negative connotations in one language can be very different when translated. Take the famous example of Mitsubishi's "Pajero" (which means *"jerk"* in Spanish).

D. Trademark registration.

You need to check that there are no other brands using the same name. Failure to do so can mean your trademark registration is blocked by another brand that wants to (and can) protect their own interests.

Personally, I recommend checking if the brand is registered in your own country and any other country you're thinking about expanding into in the future.

E. Available domain.

Given that I'm taking for granted you will market your brand online, your chosen name must be available as a domain and hopefully not already held by another person. The most important one is of course ".com", but I'd also recommend registering any national domains (e.g. ".es" if you intend to sell in Spain) at the same time.

F. Profiles available on social media.

This is not a must, but if your brand name is available for use on a variety of social networks, so much the better. If during the course of your investigation you find that the social media you're checking has availability, don't delay – register the brand name (it's free) and then you can decide later on if you need to use them or not. Of particular importance will be those that play a part in your strategy (Facebook, Instagram, YouTube, etc.).

3.1.2. Trademark registration.

A bad decision during the process of trademark registration can end up being very costly, either because you've followed the prevailing advice and turned to a lawyer specializing in intellectual property rights, or because you've decided to leave it all till later.

During the interviews conducted for my research, I came across examples of both. On a few occasions the entrepreneurs had decided to use a lawyer for their trademark registration, shelling out around $2,000 in the process, while on others, they had ruled out registering their brands because they thought it was too expensive (well, the lawyer certainly was!). It just so happens that the former belonged to the group of interviewees who turned out to in fact have significant funds, while the latter came from the group that had far more limited budgets.

Now I'd like to share my own experience with you.

Back in the day, I found myself faced with the same dilemma when it came to registering my first brand. Having visited one of these law firms (first making sure I wouldn't be charged for the consultation), it seemed that my chances of registering the brand were poor, as the minimum fees quoted by these experts was $700. And I say "minimum" because as the lawyer explained, "if everything goes well" for just $700 my trademark would be registered. The problem was that he failed to explain what exactly he meant by "if everything goes well". At my insistence he ended up divulging that the average price of registering a brand was in fact around $1,800. What a coincidence – the same sum paid by the entrepreneurs I had interviewed!

Despite the quoted price giving me an excellent reason to not register my brand through a lawyer, the ultimate reason was his failure to explain the advantages of registering my brand, with or without a lawyer.

Why on earth should I pay for his services then?

The reason I had gone to the office in the first place was because I had managed to reduce my list of potential brand names to just 3, and I wanted to find out which would have the most chances of successful registration, because if after the usual 8-15 months the whole trademark registration process takes my chosen name was not allowed, I would have to choose another and start again from scratch... and pay the full fees for registration once more. To my surprise, at this law firm they were unable to tell me which of my 3 options would have the greatest chance of success, and the best advice they could give me was to add my name to the start or the end of the potential brand names, thus ensuring successful registration. Can you imagine Applestevejobs or Stevejobsapple instead of just Apple? No, me neither.

I had followed what was apparently the correct path for an entrepreneur with sufficient funds to register his trademark, but now it was time to find out which way the path headed for a "low cost" entrepreneur.

In the event that you decide to undertake trademark registration for yourself, pay strict attention to what I'm telling you here.

First and foremost, you need to be clear about which country you want your trademark to be protected in. You can choose between national, international or community level:

- If you are only going to market your products in US, register a national brand.
- If you intend to market your products throughout the European Union, then register a community trademark outright, without the need to first register a national trademark.

- If you intend to register a trademark anywhere else, you need to have first registered it at national or community level. If you've already done so, then go ahead and start the process of registering an international one. If not, first of all register your brand on a national or community level, and once this is done and certificated, move on to the international process.

Steps to follow to register a national trademark.

1. Search for a conflicting mark.

A quick search on the USPTO[3] (US Patent and Trademark Office's) site will reveal which marks have already been registered. If a live, registered mark is similar to the one you're after, it may not be worth moving forward.

A mark must be original in spelling and/or category to be considered. For example, both Delta faucets and Delta airlines are registered marks. Even though they share the same name, they are not competitors because they operate in different industries (travel/airlines vs appliances).

---

[3] *www.soykevinalbert.com/uspto*

2. File the paperwork.

Initial application forms[4] can be located and submitted on the USPTO website.

You'll be asked to pay a $275 filing fee. Even if an application is rejected, money is not refunded.

3. Your mark either moves to the Intent-to-Use stage or receives an office action rejection.

If your application has been accepted, then the USPTO believes it can become a registered mark. In other words, lawyers have reviewed it and do not believe it will damage anything currently protected. Congrats!

When this happens, a mark moves on to the Intent-to-Use (ITU) stage.

If your application is rejected, a response form[5] can be filed. Fill out this paperwork if you'd like USPTO to recon-

---

[4] *www.soykevinalbert.com/uspto/application-forms*

[5] *www.soykevinalbert.com/uspto/response-forms*

sider and give the mark a second look. You must respond within six months, otherwise your mark will be considered abandoned.

4. The application is published in the Official Gazette.

The USPTO will publish your application in a weekly Official Gazette.

If another party thinks your mark might damage theirs, they must either file an opposition or ask for an extension of time within 30 days.

If no one protests, the mark is yours to use with a (TM).

5. Receive your Notice of Allowance and start selling!

If no oppositions occur, you'll receive a Notice of Allowance (NOA) within 12 weeks of your mark being published in the Official Gazette. Then the clock starts ticking.

You'll have **6 months to use the mark in commerce**. Once the mark has been used (i.e. a product with the mark has been successfully sold and you have proof of purchase), a Statement of Use (SOU) must be filed.

If you need more time to sell a product, you can pay a fee and file for a six month extension.

6. File the Statement of Use.

When you file a SOU, you must send pictures of the products you've been selling as well as proof of purchase (receipts, etc.).

Successfully filing the SOU will move your mark (which you've been using with a TM) from the intent-to-use stage to a full-blown, registered trademark (R)!

Beware of the unavoidable $100 SOU review fee.

7. Frame it!

If the SOU is approved, you'll be mailed an official certificate. Frame it and hang it proudly in your home or office.

To keep your trademark active, all you have to do is fill out some maintenance paperwork a few years later. The first batch is due within five to six years of receiving your official certificate; the second batch between the 9th and 10th years of owning your mark.

Disgruntled third parties can still try to cancel your mark for up to five years. After that, the trademark becomes incontestable.

What can you do if there is opposition to your brand?

1. The first thing you should know is that it is normal to find some objection to your brand. If you've done everything correctly, there's no need to worry.

Oppositions are usually filed when your brand is too similar to another already in existence, has a similar logo etc. I say 'usually' because it is surprising how many oppositions are made based on claims that simply don't stand up.

So, the question should be why are there so many opposers making nonsense claims? The reason is that many trademark holders have paid the lawyers who completed their registration process for a **surveillance service** which incurs annual fees. This means the lawyer has to justify their fees, whether there is real reason or not. Further, for every opposition lodged, they charge extra fees, over and above the annual payment of course. Not a bad business, is it?

2. Once the **USPTO sends you a notice of opposition to your mark**, your application is put on hold. This will then be published in the Official Gazette and you have one month from the date of publication to file your pleading.

Your pleading must be presented before the USPTO. You can do so in person at any physical office, via email, or post. I recommend you don't rush things and take time to get your case in order, to avoid any problems.

If on your application form you supplied an email address, before receiving this Notice of Opposition, you will get an email letting you know that your trademark registration is on hold due to the opposition of a third party.

3. You can now **download the opposing brand's list of claims** and check who is making the opposition, the distinctive details of its brand (name, logo...) and in what classes it is registered.

Normally on this claims document you'll find 30-40 pages replete with the same complex technical jargon repeated in paragraph after paragraph. Don't let this get to you. Remember that most of the time, behind these unintelligible allegations, there is just one barefaced lawyer trying to justify his exorbitant fees.

4. You can use the document you receive from the opposer and dispute the points therein that you consider essential to your defense.

Never base your claims on opinions or subjective assessments, nor on discrediting the brand that opposes yours. Analyze your opposer's arguments thoroughly, take your time to read their objections in detail and take notes on anything that doesn't sound right, as these things often make no sense.

5. Once you have filed your claims, an examiner from the USPTO will read the opposing mark's claims in detail, then your claims, and **decide whether your mark can be registered** and co-exist with the opposer or not, and whether it can do so fully or partially. This can drag on for at least two months from the day you file your answer.

Whether things are eventually settled in favor of your interests or those of the opposing brand, **both parties will now have a new one-month deadline to file a motion for appeal**. If you have won this round, you won't hear for at least a month whether the opposer has decided to appeal or not.

3.1.3. Storytelling.

Your brand name should be something capable of evoking emotional ties in the user and to achieve this, storytelling can be of great help.

Storytelling means telling a story in a way that engages with your potential customers on an emotional level.

We know that people make decisions as a result of one or more emotions, and not always in a rational way. With hindsight, we use reason to justify the decisions we made on an emotional level, and this is important to keep in mind. Storytelling seeks this emotional connection.

When it comes to creating your brand name, harnessing storytelling in the correct way can be a truly powerful weapon that you shouldn't disregard.

If there is a good story behind your brand name, one that stays etched on your (potential) clients' memories, your brand's customer retention will increase, as will diffusion to third parties.

Don't miss this opportunity to make an impression on the target audience from the word go.

The worst thing that can happen is that someone asks you what the significance of your brand name is, and you have to reply "well actually, it doesn't have one". You'll look like you could care less. You'll have missed your first chance to harness storytelling to boost your project's word of mouth.

How to use storytelling.

A. Create meaning for the name.

You probably know that Nike is inspired by the Greek goddess of victory, Niké, fitting perfectly with the brand's sporting philosophy.

We all love trivia and anecdotes, and these can spread from one person to another vitally.

B. Don't worry about looking like a freak.

Don't worry too much about coming across as weird – sometimes, the crazier the story is, the more attention it will attract. It's like when you see an ad on TV and you think "WTF?" They may think you're crazy, but at least they're talking about you.

C. Share how you came up with the idea.

People like to know how you came up with the idea for your brand name because they like to know that, behind the brand there are real people, and they want to get to know that person better, learn about their life before launching the brand. Your job situation, your friends, where you live or even what you were doing when the brand name occurred to you...they can all have a strong impact. Share your story!

D. You have to be confident.

Don't just invent a story because you think it will attract more attention. Every time you tell it, the people who listen to you should see the twinkle in your eyes. It must be a story you are 100% confident of if you want it to make an impression on your listeners.

As with pretty much everything, there are exceptions.

If in your particular case you feel that being true to yourself and telling the real story behind your brand name will only jeopardize you, it might be a better idea to grant yourself artistic license and embellish it a little.

Example:

> During a radio interview, the founder of the well known footwear brand Pikolinos, decided to tell the story of how his brand was born. As he explained it, finding himself in an Italian brothel alongside other Spanish businessmen, his attention was attracted by the word the prostitutes used to refer to him and his fellow countrymen, in reference to their small stature, and just like that, he decided to use the name to christen his company.

3.1.4. Slogan.

As you establish your brand, you should aim to define a relevant value proposition, a memorable brand promise for your audience.

Your slogan is the summary of your value proposition as a brand and forms part of your identity.

There are many factors that bolster this value proposition but one thing that will certainly help you to focus your message is a slogan or tagline – a short sentence that embodies the promise your company makes.

Slogans are a great way to arouse emotions in your potential customers, to get them to smile, make them think or give them a sample of what they can expect from your company.

Your slogan should embrace or evoke the essence of your brand, its personality and the features that make it different from other brands in the same field.

Why use a slogan?

- It helps to reinforce the brand meaning.
- It neatly summarizes your value proposition.
- It defines and distinguishes you.

What prerequisites should a slogan fulfill?

- It should be short and memorable.
- It should define who you are, what you do and why you are important to your clients.
- It should be flexible because, if not well composed, it can hamper future changes of direction.
- It needs to be timeless, given that it is a long-term strategic element of the brand.

These are many demands on one short sentence, I know, but don't worry, sometimes it can be difficult to comply with each and every prerequisite. That's OK, your slogan doesn't need to do all the hard work by itself, the most important thing for you to keep in mind is that it needs to be aligned with all the other elements making up your brand.

How can you create a powerful slogan?

A good way to get started on creating your slogan is to distill everything you've learned so far in the previous chapters, including the mission, vision, values and positioning, and try to simplify it all in a single sentence.

A. Brainstorming.

Make a list of words or concepts for each of the following categories:

- Your brand or your business.
- What you do and what products and/or services you offer.
- How you do it.
- Your point of view.
- Your personality, what you would like to convey to your clients.

Feel free to use adjectives, nouns, verbs...any word or phrase that springs to mind for each category. You can also ask friends, family, customers or acquaintances – it's always good to get a range of opinions and external ideas.

B. Choose the best words.

Next, choose 5-10 words from your list.

C. Assimilation with your name and logo.

Put your chosen words next to your brand name and logo, and check that they go well together.

Look out for any words that don't work with the name or logo, and if so, remove them.

D. Slogan creation.

Write different combinations of your chosen words in the form of short phrases. Try to distill the essence of your brand.

How will you know if you've found a good slogan?

- It makes you smile.
- It makes you rethink your way of thinking.

- It reflects your personality or attitude.
- It plays on words.
- It is concise.
- It is catchy.
- It suits the logo and brand name.
- It's different from competitors.
- It draws attention.
- It does not create confusion.
- It creates a desire or need in the reader or listener.
- It says much more than the words that form it.
- It generates curiosity.

3.2. Visual identity.

3.2.1. Logo.

A logo is the graphic representation of a brand, and as such the most conspicuous aspect of the company vis à vis the target market. It appears on the company's stationery, website, business cards, advertising, etc.

This is why you should never underestimate your logo's design, nor take it lightly, as it plays a vital role in your global branding strategy. In the same way that a well-designed logo contributes to a company's overall success, driving new clients to choose your brand over your competitors', a poorly developed logo, or the complete absence of one, can scare clients away, implying as it does a lack of professionalism. You will also diminish your chances of being the chosen brand when it comes to purchasing decisions.

Types of logos.

Although, as I will expand on later, I'm not a fan of you taking on the job of logo design for yourself, it is nevertheless important for you to understand the different types of logos out there, to be able to correctly advise your chosen designer, as well as to be able to better make the final decision from the various options he or she presents you with.

A. Wordmark logo.

B. Brandmark logo.

C. Combination marks: a combination of text and symbol that are clearly separate and can function as such.

D. Emblem: in this case, text and image are combined. They are indivisible parts of a whole and only work together.

10 characteristics of a well designed logo.

When it comes to designing a logo there are many things to keep in mind. I personally think it is too difficult to include each of them, so you will probably have to decide which ones are more important in your particular case.

1. Simple.

A logo makes an impact in just one or two seconds, so anything over-complicated will just be baffling. It's much better to work on simple designs, pared down to the max and with carefully chosen colors.

2. Legible.

Like the symbol, fonts (in general) must be clear, easy to read and if possible, customized, so that anyone can identify that particular font with the brand, even without having the logo in front of them.

3. Representative.

Your logo should reflect the values of your company and, if possible, be sufficiently descriptive of your company's activity.

4. Memorable.

To make a logo stand out from the crowd, it must be easy to remember. Your logo should immediately conjure up your brand at first sight. A logo can be considered memorable when a person has seen it only once and is able to describe it to someone else.

5. Visible.

For a logo to be remembered, it must first attract a person's attention. If the logo has no visual impact and goes unnoticed, it will be impossible for it to have a lasting impact on the consumer's mind.

6. Original.

The graphic representation of your company must stand out from others, it must have something that makes it different, unique and memorable.

7. Lasting.

When you're creating a logo it's normal to feel influenced by current trends, but for a logo to work in the long term, you should set those trends aside and go for a timeless look that won't age. Mind you, this does not mean that future modifications are not possible. Big brands such as McDonald's or Starbucks have slowly modified their logos while keeping the same basic concept, i.e. they have evolved over time.

8. Adaptable.

Logos will be used in different formats, sizes, colors, etc. meaning that at the time of creation, you should preempt each of these variables and ensure your logo is sufficiently fit for purpose no matter what, in terms of colors as well as size and shape.

Therefore, now is the time to think carefully about the different places and formats your logo will be used in (both now and in future), saving yourself time, money and headaches.

Examples:

- Stitching.
- Screen prints.
- Square and rectangular formats.
- Miniatures (web icon).
- On different colored backgrounds.
- Etc.

9. Authentic.

A logo should not be deceptive, but rather should reflect reality (or at least the positive aspects of it). It will be of little use to endow the logo with certain values if these are not reflected in the company beyond that.

10.Color.

The choice of color is crucial on a logo, meaning you need to keep in mind the different uses your logo will have and the potential versions of this to ensure it is fit for purpose on a range of media.

You should be aware that when picking your logo's colors, you are also picking your corporate colors. Don't worry, I'll discuss colors in more depth in the next section.

How do I design my logo?

To begin with, I should mention that during the course of my research, I attended various courses on "how to design your own logo" to see if they could change my mind that a logo must always be created by a professional. I would have loved it to have worked and to be able to tell you that, with a bit of practice, you too can save your cash on a designer specialized in this field. But sadly, it's not so. The aim of these courses was only ever to teach you how to use a specific design tool (Photoshop, Inkscape etc.) and that is simply not enough. Of course you can learn to sketch a specific design, learn to vectorize it and even find out about the use of certain colors to evoke the connotations you want to associate with your brand. But none of that will magically give you the talents of a professional designer, the talent needed to create a good logo.

So you may be asking yourself, "just how do I design my logo?" Or rather, "who designs my logo?"

Fortunately (for you), at this stage of the game, most business owners and entrepreneurs have an epiphany, suddenly recalling that long lost cousin who studied art or, even worse, their own skills with Photoshop. I say fortunately because, thanks to this trend, if you do things properly, you'll be various steps ahead of the game.

Your logo is going to be your brand insignia, present in each and every element/action of marketing and communications. Therefore, due to its importance, your logo should be designed by a professional.

I know we're talking about low cost branding here, and that if you've ever read or heard about the creation of a big (or not so big) brand's logo, these probably spoke of 4-6 digit sums. And truth be told, these sums are not far off those you'll see if you pop into an advertising or branding agency.

As always, to be able to state this with conviction, I carried out research first. And on this specific occasion, I also had the chance to discuss it openly with quite a few of the entrepreneurs I interviewed. One of them went so far as to confess that in his search for an advertising agency that would design his logo, he was juggling quotes that ranged between $13,000 and $30,000. In the end he approached an acquaintance who was "quite good at these things" and got it done for just $2,500. What a bargain!

So, when I recommend that you put your trust in a professional for the creation of your logo, given the high market prices, then where does the "low cost" come into it?

Remember that secret that's got the branding industry's knickers in a twist, and thanks to which I am systematically barred from all conferences on the topic?

Read carefully, because what I'm about to reveal will help you to save a lot -a LOT- of money.

THE SECRET 1/2

Right, here goes. The secret the branding agencies and many professionals in the industry don't want you to know about is the existence of **specialized marketplaces**[6] **in which you can find leading experts in design, programming, marketing etc.** for a fraction of the price that same service would cost you at a traditional branding or advertising agency.

How is this possible?

Easy: these platforms allow you to get in touch with freelancers who work from home, meaning that in your expenses you're not paying for the indispensable luxury premises that any branding agency worth its salt occupies. I mean, an agency selling branding can't afford to neglect their own, can they? You will also not be liable for the overheads and management costs of these charming, centrally located agencies: the customer service department, cleaning personnel, sales people, lawyers, managers, catering expenses and the office party, etc. This alone makes a considerable difference to the fees quoted. More importantly, however, is that **you can work with freelancers from countries whose currencies are much weaker than ours,** whose average salaries are much lower but whose level of education and training is the same or higher, **giving you the same results for much less money**.

---

[6] *A marketplace is a virtual space that puts freelancers from all over the world in touch with companies or individuals seeking talented professionals.*

THE SECRET 2/2

As if it were not enough to try to prevent you from finding out about this type of platform and thus be able to compare quality and prices to make your own decision about who to hire, many branding agencies keep an even more twisted secret... **The agencies themselves use these platforms** when they receive an order from an unsuspecting customer. In other words, you commission a logo (or any other work) from an agency, and they then advertise your job on one of these platforms as "private work" (to avoid being caught), pay even less than you would on the self same platform, because they're regular customers, with their own special terms and conditions (that you can read for yourself on the website), and at the end, deliver your commissioned piece, created by a freelancers for a very affordable price but with a couple of additional criteria. What they're doing in reality is acting as middlemen, and while charging for this service is not bad *per se*, acting as middlemen without the client knowing anything about it, and inflating the price five or tenfold, takes a lot of nerve.

So now what?

Now that you know **THE SECRET**, I'm going to show you how to use the best marketplaces for each task associating with creating a brand.

Each platform has a proprietary system and its own little tricks to get the most out of it, along with the results you're looking for.

Note: *Although there are also platforms that are cheaper than the ones mentioned below, I have decided not to include them as, once again, the aim of this book is to create a brand with the same or better quality you would achieve via a good branding agency, and not just "acceptable results".*

LOGO CONTESTS

How about if your logo was designed not by one professional, but by dozens of them, who prepared a variety of design proposals from which you could choose the one that best fits your needs and likes, then work on that chosen one until you have the perfect logo? And if you could do all that for less than $300, and your money back if you're not completely satisfied?

Well, that's exactly what's on offer on platforms such as *99designs*[7] o *Freelancer*[8].

Note: *When you access these platforms, you'll notice they offer other services besides logo design. We'll cover better options for such services later on.*

How does it work?

99designs.

1. Write a briefing for your logo.

First of all, explain what your company is all about and what the logo you're searching for looks like. Everything you have learned so far will prove useful. Take your time. The more details, the better your design options will be.

a) State what type of logos you like.

You'll be shown over 100 examples of different logos and you'll have to choose the ones that best fit you and

---

[7] *www.99designs.com*

[8] *www.freelancer.com/*

your company. When you make your decision, remember the types of logos we looked at earlier.

b) Choose your brand's style.

- Classic or modern
- Old or young
- Feminine or masculine
- Affordable or luxury
- Abstract or literal
- Etc.

Always bear in mind your brand's essence, its personality, its value proposition, what it is that you want to express...

c) Choose one or more colors for your brand.

Remember, color is highly significant in helping you to express whatever it is you want to communicate (more details in the next section).

2. Choose a design package.

The different packages on offer are rated Bronze, Silver, Gold, and Platinum.

These packages range from the most basic, for just $259, where you'll receive around 30 designs created by good designers; to the most professional at $1,199, where you'll be treated to around 60 designs created by designers hand-picked by 99designs.

Each of these packages offers a 100% money-back guarantee, as well as the full intellectual property rights. Furthermore, it's good to know that each package includes not only the designer's fees but also all taxes and commissions.

At this stage you can also make your order private for just $35 more. I'm sure you can think of a certain type of person or company this would appeal to, right?

You also have a dedicated customer service team to solve any problems and answer your queries, as well as a free design consultation.

Freelancer.

In order to compete with 99designs, the website Freelancer launched a "contest" option. Just like on 99designs, it allows you to choose not just one professional to help you design your logo, but dozens or hundreds, who will send you their proposals for you to choose from.

Setting up a contest on Freelancer couldn't be simpler. Once you're on their website, click the button "Post a project" in the top right. Describe your project, and indicate what skills the participating freelancers will need to have (examples include graphic design, illustration, Photoshop, and so on). Next, it will ask you how you want to begin the job; "Post a project" or "Start a contest". Select the "contest" option, set your budget and how many days you want the contest to last for, and whether you want it to be a guaranteed contest[9]. And that's it!

As you can see, all you have to do is select a platform on which to run your contest, and before you know it you'll have dozens of professional designers from all over the world working on different ideas for your logo – all for up to 100 times less than a single pitch would have cost you from a traditional branding agency.

Are you starting to see why branding agencies don't like me?

---

[9] *This means that you guarantee that you will select a proposal to give the award to, even if none of them totally grab you.*

3.2.2. Corporate colors.

The color(s) of a brand can have a very strong influence (60-80%) on the decision to purchase your product (or not). Each color evokes different feelings, sensations, and emotions in the human brain, making it extra important to choose an appropriate one.

That's why choosing your brand's corporate colors is such a momentous event.

Choosing corporate colors isn't just a question of taste. Depending on the type of company (or professional individual) you are, the products or services you sell, and the values you want to convey, you need to choose one color or another to attract the right customers.

Choosing suitable corporate colors in line with a well developed branding strategy helps to:

- **Convey and evoke emotions** in your target audience that go beyond the message itself. Evoke at a glance the emotions that we want the potential client to experience.

- **Differentiate you and help you stand out** from your rivals.

- **Connect** with the target audience.

What each color conveys and symbolizes (color personality).

- **Red:** An emotionally strong color, suggestive and provocative. It symbolizes passion and intensity. It is also connected to energy, and is a color that conveys a certain sense of urgency, making it useful in promoting special offers, for example. It has the ability to make your heart beat faster, and boosts appetite.

- **Blue:** Unlike red, blue is a color that transmits peace and tranquility. This is the most natural color and the one the human eye sees most often, being the color of the sea and the sky. It is also the color of masculinity. It increases trust, due to having no aggressive connotations.

- **Yellow:** Symbolizes happiness, joy, intelligence and energy. It is a youthful color, conveying positivity and clarity. It evokes pleasant, happy feelings. It fosters communication and stimulates mental processes. An interesting fact is that this color can make babies cry more. Viewed as a laid back color, it's probably not suitable for high-end products or services.

- **Orange**: Merging the energy of red with the happiness of yellow, orange is a warm color which conveys enthusiasm and excitement. It is associated with joy, the sun and the tropics. An orange logo seems friendly and cheerful. It spurs consumers to take action. It connects easily with a young audience.

- **Green**: The color of health, tranquility, the environment. The human eye can differentiate more shades of green than any other color. It symbolizes relaxation and self-care. Muted dark green is associated with money and is ideal for businesses in financial, banking and economic fields.

- **Purple**: This is the color of creativity, imagination, and also mystery. Historically, this color was commonly used by royalty hence it symbolizes wealth, power and knowledge. It is a calming color.

- **Pink**: This is the color of femininity, of peaceful energy. It conveys finesse, innocence and kindness. This is the color of the world of dreams and the imaginary.

- **White**: Suggests simplicity, purity, goodness, truth, cleanliness, hygiene, and also perfection. That's why it is commonly used by companies in the fields of healthcare and assisting others, as well as those wanting to express simplicity.

- **Black**: Represents power, bravery, elegance, sobriety, formality. For companies, it can communicate integrity and reliability.

Seeing the significance colors can have for your brand and – although at first you are recommended to let your graphic designer evaluate your company – knowing about the psychology of colors can help you to make decisions based on more than just your personal tastes.

Another thing to bear in mind when choosing colors is the audience your business is targeting. Depending on the age, sex or other characteristics of your ideal client, you should pick certain colors over others.

Internet users and consumers in general are susceptible to feeling influenced by color when making purchases, while at the same time the color produces attraction and a positive perception of some brands, and vice versa.

3.2.3. Corporate typeface.

At present, writing is still one of the most significant means of communication, hence it is also an important medium to take into consideration when creating a brand.

The aim of a corporate typeface is to apply typographic design standards to all written communications of the company, both online and offline. Thus, these rules should apply to both external communication (advertisements, brochures, catalogs, etc.) and internally (letters, delivery notes, invoices, budgets, presentations, etc.).

As with colors, picking your typeface or font is highly important. Your typeface, along with the other elements comprising your brand, will transmit the message and the values you want to communicate.

Depending on what exactly it is you want to communicate as a brand, you should pick one typeface or another.

A typeface or font should be in line with everything the company represents, and therefore should reflect the values of your particular brand.

3 basic factors to keep in mind when choosing your corporate typeface.

Although there are no set rules when it comes down to choosing your brand's font, it is a good idea to follow some basic guidelines that will help you to make a more informed decision.

1. The difference between serif and sans serif.

First off you should be aware of the differences and uses of the 2 main font families: serif and sans serif.

A serif font (Times New Roman, Georgia, Cambria, etc.) is one whose letters feature small decorative flourishes at the tips, while a sans serif font (Arial, Helvetica, Monaco, etc.) does not have these details.

In broad terms, serif fonts are chosen by printed media and we commonly see them in newspapers, books and magazines. Digital media, meanwhile, tends to prefer sans serif fonts.

Likewise, while serif fonts are commonly used by traditional businesses (consultancies, lawyers...), sans serif fonts are used in more innovative businesses or ones that aim to convey modernity.

2. The relationship between typeface and mood.

Typefaces have the power to unleash emotions. I don't mean that a certain type of letter can make you cry or burst out laughing, but yes, they can trigger emotions.

The mood your typeface induces should be consistent with your brand. Is it fun? Laid back? Fresh? Choose a font that embodies all of this.

3. Careful with combinations.

In general, you are recommended to use no more than 2 different fonts.

More is not necessarily better, especially in this instance – choosing a font.

The general rule is that you can get away with a mix of serif and sans serif. For example, using "Helvetica" for headings and "Times New Roman" for the body of the text is a safe combination and works very well.

If you're going to use a customized typeface, try to leave the text body in a font that's simpler and easier to read, and keep that original typeface that projects your brand's personality for the headings.

Note: *Decorative typefaces should be used sparingly.*

3.2.4. Website.

Your website will not only become the operations center for your online branding strategy, but will also form the basis of your digital strategy to generate revenue.

In other words, your website is the online counterpart to your shop, office, branch or physical premises in the offline world.

Thus the mission of your website should be the same as that of your physical business – a showcase to display your products and/or services, explain who you are and your value proposition, offer information and advice, transmit security and trust, create a connection hub for your clients... Of course, all with one overarching aim – TO GENERATE INCOME.

As such, it seems only logical that if refurbishing and fitting out premises for your new business costs somewhere between $10,000 and $30,000 then creating a professional website should come in at a similar price. And that is the case. Creating a good website can require the same amount of time and the same number of experts (if not more) as the refurbishment of business premises.

The online world features a number of advantages however, which – as long as you're aware of them and know how to use them appropriately – can save you a lot of money.

Imagine being able to pay off the refurbishment of the premises you've chosen for your business by partnering with another 100 entrepreneurs who will also use the space. In this way, a refurbishment that was going to cost you $30,000 now only entails you paying $300. Wouldn't that be great? There are evidently two problems with this; firstly, it would be difficult to design the premises to everyone's needs and taste; secondly, and more importantly... how the heck are you going to fit 100 entrepreneurs in one office?

Luckily, the online world is a bit different and one website costing $30,000 to create can be paid off between 100, 1000, or even 1,000,000 business people. Each person pays a vastly reduced sum and the creator profits because their work is being sold a thousand times over. We're talking about CMS and WEB TEMPLATES.

Your website for less than $500.

Let's continue to get the branding agencies' backs up.

In order to land yourself a professional website worth $30,000 for less than $500, you need just three things: a **CMS** (free), a **good theme or web template** (between $59 and $99) and a **good programmer/designer** to assemble the template ($300-400).

First of all, I want you to understand that opinions on this are conflicting. There are many experts who defend the use of CMS and web templates, while others prefer to develop their own from scratch. Both options have their pros and cons. I think the most honest thing to do is explain these pros and cons to the client and let them decide for themselves whether to (and if they can!) pay the $30,000.

Nowadays, given the upsides and downsides of each option, I would recommend in 90% of cases to use CMS and web templates, independently of the client's budget.

I won't get into the whys and wherefores, firstly because it's all highly technical and secondly because I imagine that if you're reading this book, it's because your neither have nor want to invest $30,000 on a website – and you don't have to!

I have no problem with a branding agency championing a custom-built website, and if the client can and wants to pay for it, great. But I do think it's an affront and downright dishonest to do what many branding agencies do: charge for a website as if they had custom built it, when in fact they are using CMS and templates too.

Example:

On one occasion, a client who was also a friend was telling me about the business he had just set up and how a branding agency located in Denmark had created a fabulous website for him, for which he had paid just $20,000, whereas in Spain he had been quoted double. When he showed me the site I asked him if he wanted to know the real cost of such a site. He gave me a strange look, not realizing exactly what I was talking about, but gave me the go-ahead anyway. So I accessed the website's internal coding, found out their CMS (which they had clearly attempted to hide and disguise), and found the name of the template they had used (which cost about $67). My friend stood up without saying a word, went out to the balcony and started screaming in a different language for 15 minutes. Did that mean they had scammed my friend and he would have a legal case against them? Unfortunately, not. In reality, the agency simply created the website my friend had requested for the price agreed, no more no less. So, did the agency act ethically? No way! This kind of thing happens in many sectors, not only branding, but is characteristic of unscrupulous scumbags!

1. What is a CMS?

A CMS, or content management system, is a computer application used to create, edit, manage and publish multimedia digital content in various formats. There are many types of CMS. depending on what they're used for. Some of them are: WordPress, Prestashop, Shopify, Drupal, Magento... Personally I prefer WordPress for several reasons:

- It's easy to use and manage.
- A web design in WordPress has no limits to development and expansion.
- You can add thousands of features that other CMS do not and will not offer.
- 1 out of 4 websites is made in WordPress. There must be something to it...
- 65% of websites that use content managers are designed in WordPress.
- It is specially developed to make it easier for you to rank on Google.

It should also be noted that if the designer who will set up your website recommends a different platform and gives good reason for it, then go ahead. Remember that in the end, they're the expert and if you've chosen carefully, they know what they're doing.

2. Your web template.

Although its use is not strictly necessary, using a good web template serves a dual purpose; on the one hand lighten (not eliminate) the load of design work for whoever you hire to create your website, saving you a lot of money on time spent exclusively on design; and on the other hand guarantee, insofar as possible, the correct functioning of the site (speed, positioning, etc.) and to minimize potential problems (security, updates, etc.) in the future.

I currently believe that of the 1,000s of website templates that you can buy online, you only need to worry about choosing between two: *Genesis*[10] by StudioPress and *Divi*[11] by Elegant Themes.

---

[10] *www.studiopress.com*

[11] *www.elegantthemes.com*

OPTION A: GENESIS

StudioPress offers WordPress templates based on the Genesis framework.

The Genesis Framework is a "layer of code" that makes your website work better.

Among its advantages compared to other templates that don't use this framework are its loading speed and its flawless SEO optimization (web positioning).

Prices range from $59-99.

OPTION B: DIVI

Divi is the star template/plugin of the Elegant Themes company.

Driven by the *Divi Builder* layout designer, this is a visual editor that allows you to quickly and professionally create fully customized websites.

Its main advantage is undoubtedly the speed with which its layout designer allows you to finish a web project, greatly reducing development costs.

Prices range from $69-89.

There is a heated debate on the internet about which of the two is better. There are strong camps of supporters on both sides and each has equally valid points. Personally, flying in the face of what the majority of bloggers say, I would opt for Divi, for the simple fact that it lets you develop a website in far less time, meaning your expenses will in turn be less, which is exactly what we're looking for.

Note: *Make no attempt to to save yourself this $59-99 by using a free template. You'll save yourself various headaches: security, updates, support, etc.*

3. Your web programmer.

Once you have your chosen template it's time to find an expert in the field to adapt it to your project's particular needs.

There are numerous freelance marketplaces where you can upload your proposal. Personally, I would go for Upwork[12].

It's easy to use, just follow these steps:

---

[12] *www.upwork.com*

A. Publish your project.

Give as much detail as possible about what you want and set a fixed price. Remember to include a link to your chosen web template so that the programmer can advise you on its suitability. Within just a few minutes from publishing your project, you will begin to receive offers from dozens of freelancers.

B. Compare proposals and choose your freelance.

Of the proposals that fit your budget, be sure to choose a proper professional. The first thing you should notice is if the proposal is just a copy and paste job, sent to everyone no matter the project, or if they've taken the time to respond to you personally, as well as professionally, showing interest in your project. Just by doing this you'll be able to significantly narrow down your list of offers. Now you need to take a look at their previous work and the scores and feedback left by other clients.

C. Pay "when you're satisfied".

One of the biggest advantages of these platforms is the security they offer. Imagine, for example, that you choose the wrong freelancer and end up hiring an "impostor" (some people showcase work they didn't do themselves) or you simply think that the job has not been completed as agreed. There's no need to worry, you only pay when the work is done and only if you're satisfied. Just like with a branding agency, right?

Now that you've got your website, what host do you need?

To wrap this chapter up, I am going to tell you about **web hosting**, a fundamental factor in the development of a web page and one not usually afforded the importance it deserves.

The web host is the *virtual site or space* where your website is stored. Much depends on it, among other things, the security and loading speed of your website.

There are innumerable web hosting service providers with a wide range of prices and myriad unintelligible technical specifications. I recommend you focus on two fundamentally basic points when choosing your web host: the security they offer and the quality of their technical service.

At present, having worked with many web hosting providers, I'd be pushed to recommend anything other than *Bluehost*[13]. You only need to read the feedback from their customers.

---

[13] *www.soykevinalbert.com/bluehost*

CHAPTER THREE

Video Branding

Video branding is when you use the medium of video to boost your brand's image, establishing a deep and memorable connection with your clients.

Why should you include video in your branding strategy?

As I've already mentioned, a powerful brand should be able to connect with its audience on an emotional level. Videos make such a connection easier thanks to their blend of image, music and the spoken word. Conveying and evoking feelings and emotions – so important for any brand – is much easier to achieve with video than any other medium or content type.

Including video in your branding strategy lets you increase your brand visibility, boost your renown, connect with clients, build trust, retain customers, persuade, seduce, move, woo...

It is no coincidence that big brands are investing more and more in video production and video branding strategies. Any business, regardless of size, can harness the potential of video without the pain of investing huge sums of money.

Low cost video.

Unlike what happens with logo design or website development, recording a video can not be outsourced to freelancers from "more affordable" countries for the simple reason that the work requires the physical presence of the videographer themself. And sadly, when supply is limited, prices go up. A lot. What can be outsourced is the video editing, something as or more expensive than the actual filming process.

Accordingly, I'll explain the process of video creation, splitting it into two parts: filming, and editing.

To achieve a professional final result with limited resources you will have to apply a different strategy to each of these parts.

4.1. Low cost recording.

As with all the other elements that constitute a brand, my first option was to try to hire a professional at a reasonable price.

To that end, I searched on the internet and chose 10 professionals whose work, as shown on their respective websites, made it clear that they knew what they were doing. Later on I wrote an email explaining the type of video I needed and sent it to the professionals I had chosen. The work I described was a simple video, a close up of an actor speaking directly to the camera, on a white background, lasting approximately one minute and to which a tune would need to be added in post-production.

The quotes I received ranged from $600 to $3,500. $3,500 for one minute of video! What if I had needed a longer one? Or even worse, what if my strategy included video shoots on a regular basis (as is recommended)?

This clearly required an investment that was far from my personal understanding of what low cost meant, so, without hesitation, I decided to go with Plan B: learn to create a professional video for myself.

I completed my first test shoot before undertaking any research, just to see what results I could achieve. Since, as I explained in the email I had sent to the different professionals, the video I was requesting needed a white background, in the style of many Apple videos, I looked for a white wall well lit by natural light. For filming I used a compact digital camera and for sound... I stuck my phone to my chest, just under my shirt, using masking tape.

Result: a complete and utter disaster.

The background that was supposed to be bright white looked dull gray, with my shadow visible over it. The general image quality, in spite of me believing I had excellent lighting, was full of noise. And the sound... well, best not to discuss that.

Despite my disastrous result, I had what I wanted: a decent starting point for my research. Every cloud has a silver lining after all.

Throughout my research I immersed myself in dozens of courses and tutorials, both free and paying, and sought advice from numerous friends and acquaintances who worked in the video and photography world.

Once I was done with the research, I made a second attempt to shoot the same video, using all of my new-found knowledge and skills (including outsourcing the editing part), and this time I *did* get the results I was after.

Aware of the fact that my own opinion might not exactly be partial, and to confirm that I had in fact come up with a good method of creating professional videos on a shoestring, I wrote back to the professionals who had earlier given me quotes, this time from a different email address and using the video I'd just made as an example of what I was looking for. I have to say I was not at all surprised to receive pretty much the same quotes once again from these professionals, who went so far as to attempt to justify what they obviously knew to be rip-off prices with comments such as: "a video of this quality doesn't come cheap".

Equipment you will need.

A. Camera.

If you can control the lighting you can do without a professional camera. The camera is undoubtedly the most expensive part when it comes to recording a professional video, so this is where we're looking to save some money.

By learning how to make light work for you, you can achieve great results using simply a compact camera or even better, something that you always have with you anyway: your cellphone.

In most cases, it's a good idea to use a tripod to support the camera or mobile device, for added stability. As with everything, these come in a range of prices but to start off with, are available for as low as $2.

Currently I use the *lightweight tripod from Amazon-Basics*[14] (60 inches), which can be purchased for about $19.

B. Microphone.

Although it might seem strange, your sound quality will have a stronger impact on potential clients' judgment and loyalty than image quality. Better to have a video with poor image quality that can be clearly heard, than vice versa. So be careful not to underestimate the importance of this if you're looking for professional results overall.

---

[14] *www.soykevinalbert.com/tripod*

No matter how good the camera or mobile device you're using for your video shoot, use a separate device to capture audio (although I can't recommend taping your phone to your chest) because your camera's mic is designed to capture not only the speaker's voice but also background noises, and in general we're not interested in those.

After my unfruitful attempt with the phone stuck to my chest, I tried a variety of other options including digital recorders, professional lapel mics, and various low cost recording methods I discovered on the internet. Of all the options my pick is the *RODE lapel microphone*[15], specially designed for cell phones and coming in at less than $50 or, failing that, going with the low cost version: a hands-free headset.

That's right – the ones that are usually included when you buy a smartphone. The idea is to turn these headphones into a lapel microphone, which is the type of mic you can see news anchors using, for example. To do this, take a headset you no longer use and simply cut off the part with the earbuds, leaving just the mic, which is the part that has the volume control on it. Now simply attach it near your shirt collar and use any audio recording app to record your sound.

---

[15] *www.soykevinalbert.com/rode*

Of course, you could also record the sound with a Bluetooth hands-free set, but keep in mind that the video won't be quite as professional when the hands free set is hanging from your ear, and this will also be more likely to cause interference.

Note: Don't forget to put your phone on airplane mode to avoid unexpected interruptions bang in the middle of that shot that was going soooo well...

C. Lighting.

As I've said from the start, if you can control the lighting then you can shoot high quality videos without the need to splash all of your cash on a professional cameraman. That's why I recommend investing a small sum in a basic lighting kit (around $100) which will allow you to properly illuminate both the subject and the background.

This basic lighting kit usually comprises 3 light sources that can be custom-configured depending on the needs of each video. I'll briefly cover the two set-ups I use most:

1. First of all we have what's known as **three point lighting**. This type of lighting is commonly used in interviews, where the three lights point to the subject

and the background is illuminated by the light of the room itself (natural or artificial). Composition: main light, fill light and contrast light (in this order of importance):

- **Main light:** This is the most important light. This defines the subject to be filmed.

  It is positioned on one side of the subject at a height slightly higher than that of the camera.

- **Fill light:** When used alone the main light casts deep shadows on the unlit side, making it a good idea to use a fill light to soften these shadows, without eliminating them completely.

  This light is positioned on the side opposite the main light, at approximately the same height as the camera, and set to 25-50% less power than the main light.

- **Contrast light:** This light is important because it picks out the subject from the background.

  It is positioned behind the subject, either above or below them (depending on the desired effect or personal preferences) with 25% less intensity than the fill light.

2. The second configuration is particularly useful for those situations where you need to achieve a uniformly white background, or to apply a Chroma[16].

In this configuration, two spotlights are used to illuminate the background uniformly and the remaining light is used to illuminate the subject. With this set up, the fill light is noticeably lacking, as strong shadows are created on the non-illuminated side. To fix this all you need is a reflector (around $15), or in its stead, any plain white surface such as a sheet of cardboard or a large cork board, which should be positioned on the opposite side of the subject to act as a fill light, reflecting the main light.

Points to take into consideration when choosing a lighting kit.

Firstly you should be aware that there are 3 types of lighting: daytime running lights or energy efficient lights, tungsten lights, and LEDs.

LED lighting kits are, by far, the best all round apart from their high price. I will compare only the first two,

---

[16] *Use of green or blue backgrounds to add different effects in post-production.*

taking into account features such as: the heat given off, color temperature, portability and energy efficiency.

A. Heat released.

You should keep in mind that, unlike energy efficient lights which hardly radiate any heat, tungsten lights can turn any room into a sauna, which can pose a serious inconvenience, making it important to consider this feature when it comes to buying lighting equipment.

Note: If you decide to purchase a tungsten lighting kit, be very careful when handling it during use, as it can cause severe burns.

B. Color temperature.

The color temperature of a light source (which has no connection to the heat it radiates) refers to the varying tones that light can produce, and is measured in degrees of Kelvin.

It seems that, in most cases, the best temperature to film at is 5,200 degrees Kelvin, which is the temperature of sunlight and energy efficient lights. Tungsten lights, on the other hand, have a color temperature of 3,300 degrees Kelvin, producing a warmer, more orangey effect.

Of equal or more importance than your lighting kit's color temperature it to avoid mixing different color temperatures during a shoot, in turn avoiding driving the camera crazy. This would happen, for example, if one side of the subject is lit with a tungsten bulb and the other side with sunlight coming through the window.

*Note: To avoid confusing the camera, you can use what's known as **gelatin filters**. These filters are those colored sheets, similar to cellophane, which you will have often seen placed in front of a spotlight. Thanks to these filters you can turn a warm light such as tungsten into daylight by simply using a blue filter, or turn an energy efficient bulb into warm light using an orange filter.*

C. Portability.

Despite almost all lighting kits coming with their own carry cases, this doesn't mean they are the most practical for your uses.

While tungsten spotlights, once cold, only need to be stored in their respective carry cases, with energy-efficient kits each spotlight is made up of various light bulbs that need to be unscrewed and stored, each one in a separate polystyrene casing which is in turn stored in a cardboard box. If you have to assemble and disassemble the bulbs often this can end up making you *loco*.

D. Consumption.

If you're going to record videos on a regular basis, this is something you should definitely keep in mind. An energy efficient lighting kit will consume far less energy and ultimately, considerably lower your energy bills.

For example, the *lighting kit*[17] that I chose is a tungsten kit consisting of 3x800W spotlights, giving a total of 2,400W. To achieve the same power with a low power kit we would use only 540W. So before deciding on one kit or the other, it might be an idea to do some sums.

---

[17] *www.soykevinalbert.com/lighting-kit*

4.2. Low cost editing.

Once you have recorded the video, it will need to be professionally edited and this is a service that yes, you can outsource at a low cost.

When commissioning a video editor, you need to have a clear idea of what you want – the clearer your instructions, the better the result will be and for less money, as this will reduce the need for any tweaks and adjustments later on.

Let's take a look at some of the basic features along with terms used in editing – these will prove useful when you have to describe your project accurately.

Basic features:

- **Image correction**: color adjustments, contrast, etc.

- **Sound correction**: eliminating noise, hissing etc.

- **Transitions**: normally a video is made up of several different takes. It is vital to transition from one to another at exactly the right time and with the right style. To this end, before you even begin shooting, you need to have a great script which specifies, among other things, where these transitions fit in.

Additional features:

- **Header**: you may want all of your videos to start with the same header. This can be something as simple as an animation of your logo, and can really boost your brand's retention and power.

Choose from thousands of headers for less than $10 on VideoHive[18].

- **Broadcast graphics**: those visual elements that appear at the bottom of a video detailing, for example, who the person on screen is, the content or theme of the video, etc. These come in many shape and sizes, making it important for you to choose well so that they're in line with both your brand and the content of the video in question.

---

[18] *www.videohive.net*

*On **VideoHive** you can browse hundreds of different broadcast graphics.*

- **Music**: choosing a good tune can act as a powerful piece of auditory branding, conjuring up your brand every time it plays, without having to see any images. Take your time to choose it.

On AudioJungle[19] you can access an extensive collection of royalty-free music for prices ranging from $8 to $20.

- **Special effects**: just like the transitions, if you are thinking about adding any special effects, no matter how simple these may be (including text, animated objects...) these must be clearly specified in the script that you prepare before filming the video.

Time to hire yourself a video editor!

As with the development of your website, to get your videos edited you can use the *Upwork[20]* platform, and just follow exactly the same steps.

---

[19] *www.audiojungle.net*

[20] *www.upwork.com*

This time around, in the project description section, it's a good idea to use the script you've created for the video shoot. This should indicate exactly where any transitions go and each special effect you want to include.

You should also stress that you want corrections made both in the image and sound, and include any links to openers, broadcast graphics and tunes you end up deciding to use in the project description.

Remember, for the freelancers to be able to give you a more specific quote, you need to attach all files in the project description, including the video itself and audio. If you can't upload these directly to the platform due to their size, use a storage service such as Dropbox, Google Drive, Amazon, etc. Once uploaded, just copy and paste the link to the file in the project description section. Ideally, you should include them all in one single folder and just paste the link to that.

And that's all there is to it!

If you implement everything we've discussed in this chapter, you could have your very own professional video ready for less than $200, including the lighting kit, headers, broadcast graphics, tune and editing. And from the second video onward, because now you'll only have to shell out on editing, your budget will drop to around $50-100 (depending on your chosen freelancer).

CHAPTER FOUR

Personal Branding

I couldn't wrap up this book without discussing the currently trending topic, one on everyone's lips – personal branding.

Personal branding is when the person themself is considered to be the brand. Developing a personal brand involves identifying and conveying talents, skills and characteristics in the aim of differentiating oneself and thus achieve increased success in both professional and social relationships.

As you can see, the aims are exactly the same as any commercial brand.

People who are good at managing their personal brands quickly stand out from the crowd and are perceived by society (including potential clients) to be experts in their field. For these reasons, the aim of this chapter is this: **to teach you how to come across as the expert that you are.**

5.1. The experts industry.

Since the dawn of the internet, and the democratization of information, there has been a remarkable increase in the number of experts, gurus and specialists in any given field or on any topic of your choice. If someone knows how to effectively harness the tools they have at their disposal, they can quickly position themselves as an expert in practically any industry.

Nowadays it's not enough to simply be an expert, we have to be perceived as experts by the public.

"To look like an expert you should be an expert in looking like one."
Alfonso Alcántara

5.1.1 What is an expert exactly?

An expert could be defined as someone with a **vast knowledge** of a particular subject, sector or field.

In my opinion however, such a definition is incomplete, as it doesn't encompass the type of expert that you're looking to become.

It's no good being a rock star in your field if no-one in said field or in the wider public **recognizes you as such**.

So, if we consider just one side of the equation, we'll find people who have in-depth knowledge and brilliant minds yet struggle to make ends meet and would give their right leg for a decent wage, alongside charlatans who have no idea what they're talking about but earn salaries worthy of government ministers, called to participate in every conference, debate, radio or TV program out there because, for whatever strange reason completely unconnected to their knowledge, they have managed to gain universal recognition as experts.

Although the answer to just how a charlatan or snake-oil salesman manages to position themselves as an expert is complicated, on most occasions it just so happens that these fake experts possess excellent communication skills, enough to cover up any of their shortcomings. Just think for a minute about any of our current politicians or the type of people we see every day in televised "debates". In such debates what the supposed expert knows is nowhere near as important as what they appear to know, and if they can defend their opinion (or the opinion they're asked to defend that day) in an aggressive and theatrical way, then the audience is guaranteed.

I used to have a friend who I always said should sign up for these TV debates. He truly had a gift for it. This friend could argue for hours on end on any subject, even if he had no idea what he was talking about. He was so good that this type of debate became his hobby (although he would never admit it). At one point he was arguing his opinion on a specific topic as though his life depended on it, and within half an hour he would be sitting with a different group of friends asserting the exact opposite, with just as much vehemence. The funny thing was that he had no need to agree with his own arguments. He just wanted to win the debate. Nothing more. The game made him feel powerful. A power that masked many different complexes.

A true expert, the type of expert that interests us, should satisfy both sides of the equation, with a vast knowledge of their subject area and the skills to transmit as much in a suitable way, while also being recognized as such.

5.1.2 Benefits of being recognized as an expert.

A. Clients find you.

It won't be quite as necessary to go out and look for clients, or do some cold calling, because they are the ones who come to you. Being recognized as an expert allows you to attract customers more easily.

B. You don't have to sell.

Your customers want to work with you, regardless of the price. This doesn't mean that you don't have to make an effort to sell, nor that you can do without a sales system, but it does mean that you'll find it much easier to persuade your potential clients.

C. Visibility.

The media, platforms, other professionals and companies usually mention and link the websites and content of experts making it much easier to locate them on the internet. For the expert, the result is that they achieve greater visibility and exposure online, and in turn, with their target audience.

D. Business opportunities.

An expert is also considered to be one by their business colleagues and other professionals and companies. This means you become the go-to person within your field of expertise, making it more likely that business opportunities and partnerships will come your way.

E. Social prestige.

Being recognized as an expert in your field and by your target audience allows you to enjoy greater social prestige. It is not so much that you need to make regular television appearances as you need to build a positive reputation in your sector and be recognized as a professional capable of delivering the results you promise.

5.1.3 Minimum viable expert.

Being an expert isn't black and white. There are shades of gray in there too.

The idea of turning yourself into an expert may seem as daunting as climbing Mt. Everest, but in reality it comes down to you being able to adopt a Lean approach, and create a Minimum Viable Product of yourself as an expert, acquiring sufficient knowledge to know more on a given subject that 80% of the public, and also be able to communicate this in a unique, authentic way.

Your audience.

You need to address a group that can recognize you as an expert.

You *cannot* feign it, nor turn yourself into a world-renowned expert overnight, or want the society as a whole to recognize you as such.

What you *can* achieve is to be perceived as an expert by a group to whom your knowledge or experience is more than enough. For them, you will be "their expert".

Your message.

You need to know how to communicate your message to those it addresses. Each type of audience requires a different and specific form of communication, more technical, simpler, more or less formal...

You don't have to invent the wheel i.e. do something that nobody else will touch because of its obvious challenges. What you do have to be is different and unique, transforming your knowledge into a message tailored to your style and personality.

"Even the great experts are inspired by other experts."
Homer Simpson

5.2. Recognized expert in less than 30 days.

As we've already agreed, you don't have to be the world's leading expert, you just need achieve the minimum level needed to be *perceived* as an expert by your audience, and thereby be able to achieve your professional objectives.

The first thing you should do to position yourself as an expert is to BE ONE.

The aim of this section isn't to show you how to become an expert, rather, to make you aware of **how to position yourself as one**, and if possible, in record time.

To do so you need to focus on gathering the largest number of "credibility indicators".

Below you will find 5 highly effective indicators which are easy to achieve:

1. Become a member of two or three organizations in your sector of interest.

Have you ever been impressed to hear or read about a certain professional belonging to who knows how many different national and international associations and organizations? You probably thought "wow, what a machine!" and immediately mentally filed said person away as an expert in a specific field, right? Well, let me tell you a secret: to be a member of many organizations you don't need to meet a series of strict requirements. All you do is fill out a form and, in most cases, pay your monthly subscription.

Now you just have to spread the good word. Add these organizations to your business cards, your website and your social media profiles.

Could there be a quicker and easier way to be perceived as an expert?

2. Read the 3 best-selling books in your field, summarize them on one page and share these via your social media.

Creating content is laborious but distilling information and sharing it with your own personal flare is much easier to do.

If you already have enough experience in your sector and you've made sure you're properly trained and informed of everything to do with your industry, then you'll already have read these books. If you also have the good habit of underlining or highlighting sections as you read (if you don't do this, I can highly recommend you start), it won't take you more than a couple of hours to come up with a good overview of each tome.

Now all that's left to do is decide how to share the content: you can do so in an article and publish it on your blog, create a downloadable PDF to offer in exchange for the email addresses of potential customers who reach your website or (my personal favorite) create a video tutorial for your YouTube channel.

3. Start speaking at conferences.

Getting up on stage will instantly afford you the aura of expertise, and if you also prepare a great presentation supported by an attractive PowerPoint display (or any other presentation software), recognition is guaranteed.

Start by looking for events relevant to your subject area and offer to contribute by giving a talk or presentation.

You can also think about starting off at the local university, groups or associations in your line of work, or ones that have an audience similar to your target client profile. Offer to give a talk, hold a workshop, a technical seminar... anything that lets you put your knowledge on display. Explain that you'll deliver the talks for free and they don't involve selling any products or services. And don't forget to mention that you belong to the associations from point 1. When you get the go-ahead, advertise the event to all and sunder. Use your social networks, as well as forums, web page, posters, brochures, etc.

If possible, try to film the event, ideally from 2 different angles and with good quality audio (use the lapel mic that we already learned how to make). Now you've got awesome content for your YouTube channel. Make sure every last person knows that *you* are one of the experts doing the rounds at conferences ;)

4. Offer to write one or two articles for specialized magazines within your sector.

My advice is to be careful about how you approach the topic you're writing about, as a magazine will not allow you to go against the interests of their advertisers. If this means going against your own brand values, then skip this step – in the long term it could come back to haunt you. I've had to turn down offers to contribute to more than one magazine or association for this very reason.

Of course, once your articles have been published, it's okay to go ahead and announce that you're a "contributor to X magazine". This always goes down well.

5. Interview other experts in your field.

You're unlikely to find it difficult to get interviews with a good variety of professionals in your field. Most experts will happily spend the day talking about their opinions or explaining the long and winding road to get where they are today.

The good thing about interviewing an expert is that you absorb part of their "power". If people start seeing your name alongside the best professionals in your sector, they will quickly start to see you as another expert too. What is more, interviews published on your blog and suitably promoted on social media will bring you visibility, drive traffic to your website, and send your content viral.

You can carry out interviews in person or via videoconferencing, and publish them later in text, audio or video format. If you're well organized and film the interviews, you'll redouble the advantages, as not only will your name appear next to the expert's, but people can also see you chatting together like old friends.

Create a YouTube channel

Why should you have your own YouTube channel?

- It's free and it won't take you more than 10 minutes to set up.
- You can reach anyone anywhere in the world, 24/7.
- It is the second most used search engine after Google.
- It is much easier to rank on top of the search results (web positioning) on YouTube than on Google.
- You don't have stick to filming exclusive content for your channel (although I recommend you do), you can also upload videos of your conferences, interviews with experts, TV appearances etc.

- It makes you more human, more accessible, in turn facilitating trust and harmony with those who watch and listen to you.
- It allows you to transmit emotions, motivation and enthusiasm.

In spite of these obvious advantages, very few professionals and companies actually bother with this medium.

The only thing holding them back from using this powerful tool is, in most cases, their head. Shame, fear, worrying about "what they will say", modesty, an inferiority complex, peer pressure, exposure to criticism... The list of mental barriers goes on and on. However, this should give you another reason, perhaps the best one yet, to plunge headlong into creating your own videos – if you can overcome the mental barriers, YouTube offers you an excellent means to differentiate yourself, and stand out from the crowd that cowers in fear and insecurity when it comes to making their own videos.

In this book you have so far learned to create professional quality videos with minimal expenditure, so, **you can't afford NOT to have your own YouTube channel**.

5.3. Experts vs snake-oil salesmen.

First off I'd like to explain what I understand by snake-oil salesmen. As explained in previous pages of this chapter, a snake-oil salesman is an expert in looking like an expert, without actually being one. It seems like a play on words, but I assure you that they occur more frequently than you think and my aim is make you aware of how to identify this type of person, as well as ensuring you don't turn into one

Sometimes it proves useful to know how to identify these frauds, as you can then avoid hiring mediocre workers or services, you can expose your competitors, and save a great deal of money on conferences, courses and talks that will ultimately be of no benefit whatsoever.

First sign of a snake-oil salesman:
They buy their fans, followers, likes, etc.

You may ask yourself what the point of buying fans is.

Oddly enough, many people consider the number of followers a person has to be a sure-fire measure of how professional they are. Thus, many media outlets pick which expert they will call to talk about a certain topic based on this number.

Managing to create content that is interesting and different, that attracts and generate excitement among thousands or even millions of fans or followers is no easy thing, and, it goes without saying, won't happen overnight.

There are many companies that market themselves and their products/services based on purely the number of followers they have. You can – without any effort and minimal economic outlay (less than $10 for 100 followers) - achieves results that would otherwise required hard work and excellent social media strategy.

How can you tell who bought their fans?

A. Little interaction or engagement.

For some strange reason certain social networks offer less and less information from which to garner data on whether a page's followers are real or not. Luckily we can use engagement, in other words, real connections with users, as a measure. This connection can be literally measured using the percentage of interactions (number of likes, shares, comments, retweets, favorites, etc.) a page has compared to its total number of followers.

For example, is you notice a page has 50,000 followers yet only a handful of users interact with their content, you're most likely looking at fake fans (the majority of them at least).

B. Nationality of the followers.

It would be logical for followers to be of the same nationality ("most popular city" on Facebook) as the fan page itself. If my page is located in Spain, it makes no sense if most of my fans live in Bangkok.

C. Followers' age group is inconsistent.

This data can be relevant if it strays from the norm. But what is the "norm"? Well, that depends on each page. A rare example would be to find a brand for.

D. Graphs with "spikes".

On social media sites that allow you to access the metrics of a profile that isn't yours, you can find out whether said profile has bought its fans, with a high level of accuracy, by taking a look at their graphs. A page that purchases fans usually features very sharp angles in its graphs, typical of this type of practice, since paid fans tend to be added over the course of a few hours and not progressively. In such cases, you can see spikes with significant increases in the numbers of followers. On some pages you can see the increment in the number of followers from one day to the next, simply by hovering the cursor over different points on the graph.

I personally follow my competitors closely, and I have screenshots of most of their graphs demonstrating that they pursue a "strategy" of regularly buying their followers. I have to say that, contrary to what is often expounded regarding Google, Facebook or YouTube's censuring of such practices, I've never seen any of the pages I've "caught in the act" of buying fans being penalized in any way. That doesn't mean, however, that I recommend the practice.

Second sign of a snake-oil salesman:
They never speak about their competitors.

If a company or professional never mentions their competitors, DON'T TRUST THEM.

I can assure you that if someone never mentions rivals it's not because none exist, rather, they are scared you'll find out about them and switch allegiance.

I'll give you two clear examples I often encounter:

Example 1:

Have you recently attended any conferences or events on online branding or marketing (SEO and SEM, content writing, web design and development, etc.)? Did any of the "expert" speakers mention the existence of sites such as Freelancer, Upwork or 99designs, for example?

In my own experience, at such conferences it is very, very rare that any of the speakers has the courage to mention these platforms (i.e. their competitors).

Why not?

As I've already noted, these conferences usually have one aim only – acquiring new clients for the expert speaker or speakers. And of course, surely, if the attendees knew the existence of platforms that allow us to get in touch with millions of professionals from the same sector and level as the speakers, but at significantly lower prices, these "experts", who offer no added value, would run out of business.

If you ever offer to speak at any such event, it is highly likely you will be banned from speaking about these websites (I'm talking from personal experience here). And if, despite the warnings, you ignore the ban, then you can kiss goodbye to ever being invited back. Or worse still, the other speakers might harass you online and try to discredit you.

Example 2:

As a branding expert I like to follow various businesses and professionals within my field via their social media profiles.

It can be incredibly frustrating to dedicate my time to commenting with my opinion or point of view on some of the articles they publish, only to see it removed immediately.

It's not that they don't like their followers participating and commenting, as long as they can demonstrate their superiority within the subject area in question. Under no circumstances will they let their customers or follow-

ers find out about other professionals who they themselves consider to be better.

So, if you follow a so-called "expert" who never mentions any of their colleagues (competitors) in any of
their posts or articles, unless it's to disparage them, you
are most likely looking at a fraud.

*When you are – or believe yourself to be – average, the
worst thing that can happen to you is your target audience discovering your competitors.*

Third sign of a snake-oil salesman:
**They defend radical points of view and tend
to raise their voice as their preferred weapon of debate.**

I'm pretty sure that will ring a bell, right?

Indeed, this type of expert is highly valued on television, where "experts" have sprung up like mushrooms,
partly because they are needed to fill holes in the programming schedule, and partly because it is a format that
works out fairly cheap (almost free).

This way, everybody wins: the TV stations fill their
schedules at a great price and the snake-oil salesmen are

able to position themselves as the experts they can only dream of being. Because when you've appeared on TV once, everyone sees you as an expert and the press and radio will take start sniffing around.

The easiest way to get called to appear on TV and ensure you're a go-to person for their programs is simple: ATTACK. The more self-assured you portray yourself, and the more aggressively you defend your ideas, the more likely you are to become a TV expert.

Who cares if it has been demonstrated that the true experts tend to come across as more sensible, admitting that everything can have multiple approaches, and don't view a debate as an opportunity to attack the other side with the sole objective of taking the high-ground and, where possible, ridicule them. Common sense doesn't sell, and if you don't sell, you won't be asked invited back on the show, meaning nobody will hear your voice i.e. you're no longer an expert.

Fourth sign of a snake-oil salesman: They constantly spout technical jargon.

Don't let yourself be taken in, if you attend a conference or you have an appointment with a specialist and you leave feeling dumb, it's probable you've just met a snake-oil salesman.

A true expert knows how to adapt their language to their audience. Their main aim isn't to come across as an expert at all costs, but to make themselves understood and convey their message and knowledge.

Fake experts try to cover up their shortcomings, deficiencies, and lack of knowledge with a ton of complex jargon that they've memorized.

A snake-oil salesman worth his salt will use this jargon while pretending not to notice that they're using terminology only suitable for industry experts. But they do, they *do* realize, and they love how that makes them feel. You could say their aim is to impress the audience, nothing more.

"Mortgage-backed securities, subprime loans, tranches - It's pretty confusing right? Does it make you feel bored? Or stupid? Well, it's supposed to... (they) love to use confusing terms to make you think only they can do what they do or even better, for you just to leave them the fuck alone"
The Big Short (2015)

Fifth sign of a snake-oil salesman:
They never mention results.

They get up on stage and talk to us about how to get money, customers, fans, engagement, residual income, make a living from cross stitch... Any topic will do for a good snake-oil salesman.

When you meet one, don't hesitate – go right ahead and **ask them about results**.

Whether you're in a private meeting with the so-called expert or seated in the audience at a conference, don't hold back – ask them.

If they're preaching about how to generate fans on Facebook, find out how many fans they or their company actually have. If they're explaining how to increase engagement, access their social media profiles and check for yourself what percentage of interactions their posts receive. If they're trying to convince you that you can make a living from cross stitch, politely inquire about their turnover / monthly profits.

Good snake-oil salesman will come prepared with a strategy to avoid answering these questions directly, or may even just invent an answer. But you'll be surprised by how often the snake-oil salesman wishes the earth would just swallow him up right there when you ask about results.

"Those who can, do. Those who can't, teach."

Anonymous

CHAPTER FIVE

Branding for $0

What? It's possible to do branding without spending single cent? Why didn't you start there?

Well, I wanted to leave what I consider to be my best piece of advice to the end, for two reasons: firstly because, unlike all of the other chapters, this option won't work for everyone; and secondly because, even if you decide to follow the strategy I'm about to propose, it'll do you no harm to understand the tricks and tools you've been learning about so far.

You may be wondering which tool is the one that allows you to manage your branding for $0, right?

It's much simpler than you can possibly imagine:

COLLABORATION

There are branding agencies (now that we're talking about collaboration you don't need to exclude any agency on the basis of prices) which – if you present them with a good project, accompanied, where possible, by a strong business plan – may be willing to carry out all aspects related to managing your brand in exchange for a share of the profits. In other words, if *you* win, the branding agency wins, and if for whatever reason the project isn't successful, you won't have spent a single cent on branding.

As you can see, this advice, as I said before, is not applicable to everyone, because it requires a certain type of project with well-argued revenue forecasts and in which, among other things, turnover can be controlled and easily measured.

You may be thinking to yourself "Well, with everything I've learned in this book I can create and manage my brand for very little, so I prefer not to share my profits with any branding agency". And you would be right. If your only reason for collaborating with a branding agency is to save yourself that small sum of money, then this would be a very bad deal for you. But if you analyze it in-depth, you'll find that there are at least 2 good reasons why you should at least give it a go.

Reason number 1: Validate your business proposal.

Remember that a good branding agency works with dozens of clients, usually from a range of groups and sectors. Therefore, regardless of whether they have a staff member who specializes in creating and managing businesses, their vast experience working on a wide variety of projects affords them an almost prescient vision of the viability of any new project that lands on their desk. Thus, if you ask a branding agency to take on board your project as a collaborative partnership and they agree, it's pretty much guaranteed they believe it has sufficient potential to work and generate attractive returns for both parties. Likewise, if they turn down your offer, this "may be" a sign that there's something wrong with your project.

Warning: That a branding agency rejects your proposal of collaboration does not mean to say that your project will fail. There are many reasons why they might turn you down: they don't take on any collaborative work, invoicing might be difficult or impossible to control, the business may not be scalable, etc.

Lastly, if they do happen to say no, remember to ask them why. In other words, **ask for feedback**.

If you get them to defend their refusal, you will be harvesting extremely valuable information for you and the future of your project.

Reason number 2: Increase your profits.

My experience tells me that when an entrepreneur considers going into partnership with a branding agency, and said agency demands, let's say, 20% of the profits, the entrepreneur performs a quick mental calculation of how much he or she would earn every month if things go well and, thereupon, quickly rules this out as an option... when they don't even have the capital to manage their branding on a budget.

Why? Easy. If you think that your business will make, say, $3,000 per month and the agency will take 20% of that $3,000, in just 2 months you will have paid more than it would have cost you to do the branding yourself, following the advice learned in this book. And you'd be right.

So, where is this increase in profits?

A. On-going optimization.

If you stop to think about it, you'll realize that however professional a branding agency may be, they'll never take the same interest in a brand that will only bring them profit when it goes well, and in this case, depending on how well, as they would in a brand that they'll earn money from no matter what.

I'm not saying that they'll do a poorer job than if you weren't in partnership but, do you really believe anyone is going to update your website after a few months if the image this conveys is becoming outdated, that they will optimize the layout of the various elements to boost customer conversion rates, or measure the performance and impact of your various marketing campaigns (to give just three examples) if you're not paying them to do so?

And the most important thing is not whether you're willing to pay for these "extras", but that often you won't even realize that these actions are important to grow your brand and your business if you don't have a good partner alongside you, guiding you on the road.

B. Focus.

If to everything we've said so far, we add that the peace of mind that comes from having an expert branding partner lets you sit back and stop worrying about brand management, to focus on what is truly important – your job as CEO of the company – your revenue potential increases exponentially.

Let's put it another way: **do you prefer to earn 100% of $3,000 or 80% of $30,000?.**

"If you want to go fast, go alone; if you want to go far, go together".
African proverb

Things to keep in mind before formalizing any collaboration.

- Don't rush to close a deal, and carefully discuss each clause. It is advisable to seek the advice of a lawyer to be able to tie up all of your project's present and future loose ends.
- Clearly define your business model to understand where your revenue will come from. It's not the same to give a % of profits that come solely from the

sale of professional services – which depends on the amount of time spent and your fees – as to have an e-commerce with scalable turnover.

- If in doubt, ask. Never keep doubts to yourself, or do anything out of ignorance. Research, ask, and ask again. Only then can you make the best decisions.

Conclusions

I hope that reading this book has given you the push that many of us entrepreneurs need to stop us from putting off brand management until later.

If you recap, you'll find that in the worst case scenario (when collaboration isn't possible), we've managed to reduce an average budget of between $30,000-60,000, as quoted by a majority of branding agencies to create a corporate brand, to less than $1,000:

- Drafting of your mission, vision, values and positioning: $0
- Choice of name: $0
- Trademark registration: $275
- Creation of slogan and storytelling: $0
- Professional logo: $259
- Choice of typeface and corporate colors: $0
- Website design and development: $400-500

* Plus, creation of a recording studio (image, sound and lighting): $100

And most importantly, without losing one iota of quality or professionalism.

With all these new tools in your tool belt, you now have the edge when it comes to competing and standing out above all those companies who decided to ignore their branding or leave it for later. Make the most of that, and make the difference!

If you have any questions or would like to send me your comments personally, you can drop me a line at _hola@soykevinalbert.com_ I would love to get to know you, and find out a little about you and your project.

Best wishes and the best of luck, fellow entrepreneur!
Kevin Albert

Important

Like all my books, this is a beta version, meaning that it will keep improving over time and with experience. To help this to happen, I need your opinion.

Please *leave an Amazon review* for me and let me know what you thought. What did you like best? Is there anything you feel is missing? Would you add anything in, or take anything out?

Scan and leave a review

Printed in Great Britain
by Amazon